ABOUT THE AUTHOR

CW00662532

Key is now 38 years old and has pro_____ __ _____
in April 2012 in Melbourne, Australi_ ___ _____ _____
This snapped his toe, and his resultant new stance gradually gnawed
away at his spine. In spite of his poor health he has plugged away with
his poetry and his Instagram account is now booming. He has also
wormed his way into Alan Partridge's affections as Sidekick Simon
and Radio 4's affections as himself, with a third series of *Tim Key's Late
Night Poetry Programme*. He and his Dutch friend have continued to
film short but sweet incarnations of his verse, which they are trying to
get on YouTube. Amongst all of this he has been fisting various desks,
demanding this paperback be made. So this object represents a huge
victory for Key.[*]

◇◇

[*] I've got a new publisher now, a lady called Jenny Lord, who I obviously
think the world of; but to a certain extent it's still the same old bullshit.
Having to write vacuous summaries of my life and career on flaps of
paper. It can be fucking depressing. I sent her a long email, which lost
its way about halfway through and which she never replied to. But the
thrust of it was that with me, as with a lot of poets, people will either know
me or they won't, and it won't do much good trying to explain who I am
or bringing up my connections with Alan Partridge. Basically the poems
have to speak for themselves. Whenever I say things like that in meetings
she looks very sad and bows her head and my literary agent has to feed her
more coffee and biscuits to get her going again. I sometimes get paranoid
that she doesn't like my poems at all. Once I asked her outright. I said
to her, 'Listen, Old Fruit, do you like my poems or not?' She pretended
her phone was losing reception and began a nasty piece of theatre where
she was pretending to be 'cutting out'. Other times she says to me, 'Tim,
would I seriously be publishing it if I didn't like your stuff?' That always
makes me feel warm inside when she says that. I can't think that she
would be. And that gives me strength.

ALSO BY TIM KEY

25 Poems, 3 Recipes and 32 Other Suggestions. (An Inventory).

Instructions, Guidelines, Tutelage, Suggestions, Other Suggestions, and Examples Etc: An Attempted Book by Tim Key (And Descriptions/Conversations/A Piece About A Moth).

THE INCOMPLETE
TIM KEY

CANONGATE
Edinburgh · London

First published in Great Britain in 2011 by Canongate Books Ltd,
14 High Street, Edinburgh EH1 1TE

This edition published in 2015 by Canongate Books

1

Copyright © Tim Key, 2015

The moral right of the author has been asserted

Fair play to the guy – never easy to write a book.

www.canongate.tv

British Library Cataloguing-in-Publication Data
A catalogue record for this book is available on
request from the British Library

ISBN 978 1 78211 679 0

Some people go through their whole life without writing a book.

Illustration on page 256 by www.sebantoniou.com

Illustrations on pages 39 and 154 © CSA Images/Archive

And even though it's just poems, it still counts as a book.

Printed and bound in Great Britain by Clays Ltd, St Ives plc

To my decorator and his wife

NO CONTENTS[1]

<hr />

[1] There isn't a contents page per se. I obviously flirted with the idea of having a contents page and even mocked a couple up but they were, to be fair to them, very poor. And, increasingly, I found that I was becoming disillusioned with the concept of contents pages as a whole. I had drafted a vague contents page and saved it as a document on my computer (I have a white computer that I bought in America when I flew there to pursue a girl who ultimately wronged me) but every time I opened it up I was physically repulsed by the splosh of page numbers and names of poems, and nine times out of ten I threw up. Ultimately my flat/local cafés were becoming so regularly sluiced with my unhappy vomit that I decided it was best just to CTRL A and delete the whole damn lot. Anyhow, contents pages are a waste of time. So fiddly and prosaic. A bunch of disconnected words that send you into a daze and barely tell you anything of any interest. If you really want to know, the good stuff's about two thirds of the way through. Page 64's worth a look. Other than that it's pretty basic stuff. The book really doesn't warrant a contents page. And anyhow, there are indexes spread over fourteen pages at the back of the book if you're that keen on finding something in particular.

'SUNDAY MORNING'

'I never shot her,'
Ned lied.
Mr Ward cradled his dog in his arms.
His knees bent under the weight.

INTRODUCTION

P oetry, paperback. Paperback, poetry. They sound nice next to
one another, don't they? The words 'poetry' and 'paperback'.
Like 'cherries' and 'jam'. They make a merry couple.

And when the idea first came about to commit my poetry to print
I have to say I dreamt immediately of the finished book being in
paperback. There is a certain beauty, a timelessness about paperback
books. I remember my father sitting me down and telling me tales
of his paperback copy of Ted Hughes poetry. He'd go watery-eyed
as he reminisced about long, hot summer's days in the late 1950s
cycling around the Fens with a slim copy of Hughes's efforts tucked
into the inside pocket of his blazer. The sun on his back, the wind in
his hair, whizzing down country lanes, and occasionally stopping,
breathless and exhilarated, and leaning against a tree.

Miles away from any civilisation and years away from things
like Channel 4 or The Internet, the boughs of some docile oak
splooshing him into shade, my father would pull his flask from
his satchel, pour himself a cool squash and set about Hughes
like a maniac. Then, once he was done, it would be a case of flask
back into satchel, paperback back into pocket, backside back onto
saddle, plimsoll back onto pedal and away. Back home to mother.

And that was how it was.

Poets spinning their yarns, humans – like my father – enjoy-
ing their words. But it wasn't just their words. No, it was also the

format that my father and his contemporaries were beguiled by. They were in love with the wiles of the paperback. The softness, I suppose. The yield that the paperback brings to the table. The give. That's what my father talks about the most. He'll sit there in floods

these days, remembering how he could bend his Hughes clean in half. 'The give,' he'll sob. 'I appreciated the give.'

So, when I originally put together this compilation of poems and thoughts in 2011, I had sky-high hopes that it, too, would be paperback. And you can imagine it was a little difficult to take when I was told my poems were going to be slung into a hardback. Of course, my publisher at the time was a lovely man and I don't blame him for it. His name was Nick and I can honestly say I have *never* enjoyed a man's company as much as I did Nick's. We went for maybe two full English breakfasts and something in the region of five coffees over the course of our poet/publisher relationship. But the fact was he was a slave to his industry. The situation was that there was pressure to make this thing a hardback. That was how it was gonna be and we just had to wear it. We had to, in his words, 'go hard first' and we also had to, again in his words, 'suck it up'.

But I didn't want it to be a hardback. So for me it was a hammer blow.

I hate hardbacks. Big, cumbersome old sods. They piss me off no end. I can't get inside the mindset of someone who likes hardbacks. It's like these pricks who drive around on tractors or wear armour. Why would you do that? They have no place in 21st Century Britain in my honest opinion. I don't know what irks me the most, the fact that the first thirty feet of most bookshops is dominated by those bulky great artefacts, or the fact that there are twats out there buying them. Anyhow, I put all this in an email to Nick and he wrote back reiterating that that would be how it would be and asking me to explain what I meant about the armour thing.

And so it was. We were going hard. And I compiled it. And Dave designed it. And someone whose name I don't know printed it all out, and then some absolute bastards glued hard bits all round it and it went into the shops. And that would have been where you saw it last. You probably picked it up, you might have leafed through it, you will have become angry at its weight and awkwardness and you will have slid it back into its position between Keats and Kipling. After that, God knows, maybe you will have waddled to the cookery section; leafed through an Oliver.

Either way, that was where the first chapter ended. The hardback phase. I am looking at one of those books now. It is on the coffee table in my Airbnb. A big, heavy, rancid piece of work. I push it around the table with my heel. My face is on the cover. I look down at my face. My face peers back up at me. It's four years down the line. I'm moving on.

From nowhere, when it seemed for all the world that a paperback would never emerge from the hardback's grim shadow, a lady by the name of Jenny stepped up and pulled the fat out of the fire. Smart and energetic, this Jenny has done the impossible. She has outwitted the book industry. She's sent the right emails to the right people and she's nodded at the right times and she's winked at the right times and she has been a trooper. And, as a result of all of this, she has, from nowhere, magicked a paperback out of her arse!

And so here we are. Or rather here you are. Lucky enough to be clutching something svelte. In your hands are all the poems from the hardback, plus three new ones that I have eked out of my quill and dripped into the manuscript over the past three years, and all of it contained in this featherweight tome. This giving, yielding volume. This *paperback*.

INTRODUCTION

I am writing this introduction in a quaint little Airbnb in the Cotswoldshires, UK. I've escaped. I've wriggled free from the menacing clutches of London in order to track down some peace and quiet, and the best I could find is here. It is, in case you didn't know, crucial for a writer to find these favourable conditions. If he intends to write seven introductions and a new poem and generally reread and correct typos as he moves forward from hardback to paperback, it is *vital* that he finds a nice little spot to do it in.

I obviously don't want to bore you with the ins and outs of my *process*. I was once approached at a theme park by someone who was fixated on finding out all about my *process*. 'I'd be fascinated to know what your *process* is,' he kept saying. 'Come on, son, tell us about your *process*.' He was horrible, this fella. He kept breaking away from his wife and running over to me and my group. Trying to sit next to me on rollercoasters. Generally being a pain in the backside. And all the while using this word 'process' like it was going out of fashion. In the end I had to just tell him. I let him sit next to me on the Collossus and I talked him through it. Told him how I approached writing poetry. But by that point he seemed to have tuned out. Some kind of latent human instinct had kicked in and he screamed through most of what I had to say. Not that I minded. I waited till we landed and picked it up again in the bit where you can buy a photo of you screaming in the drizzle. 'The most important thing,' I confirmed, 'is that you give yourself the best conditions to write in.' And I genuinely believe that.

If you're serious about knocking out a book, or anything, really. A mag, a journal, a poem, a song, a Post-It. Whatever it is, you can't expect to be able to do it if the conditions aren't up to snuff. I demand the right temperature, the right music, the right biscuits, the right time of day. I sometimes lie awake at night wondering how that old-school bell-end Hitler managed to get his book done in prison. I just can't wrap my head round that one. If I'm sat in my own excrement in a titchy cell, wearing some kind of dowdy boiler suit, I'm getting fuck all done. I need to be in a comfortable jumper and I need to be able to come and go as I please. Which is precisely why I've forked out X amount of money, slapped my fat arse on a train for two hours and squeezed myself into this Airbnb. And believe me. It ticks the boxes.

It really is bliss being here. Just to give you an idea of the kind of place we're dealing with, it is absolutely *riddled* with beams. They are low and quaint and have the effect of making me plunge my fist into my hand and whisper the word 'nice' every time I become aware of one. The fire is roaring away. The owner – a Charles Moore – must have come up here over the weekend and stooped over his chopping block because there are something in the region of 500 chunks of wood balanced temptingly on either side of the fire, ready to be incinerated for my pleasure. And that is exactly what I'm doing. No sooner have I shat out a paragraph than I plod across to the fireplace and clumsily sling another gnarled log on. And then whoosh! The whole place lights up. And back I go, back to my laptop. Back to my wine.

Whenever you use an Airbnb I think you should feel at liberty to tuck into anything they've not locked away. I started by helping myself to a cheeky pinchful of salt last night as I boiled up some pasta for my tea. I firmly believe he'd left that salt out for that exact purpose. But today I've made myself much more at home. I've lit the bastard's candles, I've infiltrated his wardrobe, I've wrapped one or two ornaments in tea towels and squirreled them away into my overnight holdall. I have, as per his welcome pack, 'made myself at home'. And now here I sit, reclining deep, deep in his sofa, relaxing in a huge pair of his cords, and *writing*.

Writing, writing, writing. Once or twice I will pause to glug this rich stiff-neck's wine from a tankard I found hanging above the hearth. Occasionally I will sling another log on or take a dump in the ornate upstairs bog, but primarily I write. Unchallenged, without distractions. I am laying into my intros like a man possessed. I am getting the job done. I am transforming, updating, revolutionising the top and tail of my book. And I thank the advent of Airbnb and the dope they've hooked me up with for providing me with the perfect conditions in which to do it.

INTRODUCTION

Writing isn't easy. People sometimes make the mistake of thinking it is. They make the mistake of thinking any old Tom, Dick or Harry can do it. They look at a book or a text message and they think: 'I could do that.' In actual fact they are wrong. Throw these twats a pen and a ream of paper and they'd go pale, a lot of them. Because writing is tough as hell.

Being a writer is, if anything, a curse. Sometimes I'll spend maybe half an hour, forty-five minutes staring at a blank sheet of paper, my Mitsubishi Uniball Pencil swinging gently above it, clueless as to what I should write. Sometimes, after maybe two hours, perhaps longer, I will rise from my seat and sling my cushion hard against the wall of my study. That's what it can do to you. It can tear you right up. Then I'll pick up my swivel chair and smash it down repeatedly on the step next to my French windows. I'll shout as I do this. Each time I bring it down I'll yell some kind of grubby obscenity. My hands will be bleeding by this point, like that little twerp from the movie *Whiplash*, but I won't care, I'll just keep smashing my damn chair down with great force until all I'm basically left with is the stem and the wheels. Then I'll throw that against the French windows. If they smash, they smash. If they don't, I'll pick up the stem and the wheels and I'll go again. If we're still not making any inroads into the french windows, I'll take a break. I'll go and fix myself a coffee, calm down a bit, maybe have a dark chocolate biscuit or some Red Leicester. Then I'll put on a gardening glove, come back into my study, pick up the stem and the wheels of my swivel chair again, take a *huge* breath, and then I will make sure it goes through those french windows *by any means possible*. And when it does I'll collapse back onto my reindeer-skin rug and I'll groan.

Writing is hard. I know there are other jobs that are hard. You probably have one. You're probably standing there in your fire-fighter's kit right now, leafing through this with your huge heatproof gloves. A cup of coffee on the go, sucking up some verse in between the blazes. I have the utmost respect for your kind. I wouldn't run into a burning house for all the tea in China. In fact, the merest whiff of smoke and I'm out, off running the other way. Stood in the street in my dressing gown, cheering you brave boys on from the sidelines. And it's not just you. I could name ten jobs which are universally accepted as being harder than what I do for a living. Paramedic springs to mind. Top chefs constantly tell us about the stress they go through. 'It's not all about dunking our fingers in sauces and checking they're salty enough,' they say. Then there are things like teachers, trawlermen and florists. Farmers even like to get involved in the debate. The early mornings. The squeeze they feel from the supermarkets. The challenge of staying on top of personal hygiene. Everyone has it tough, I appreciate. But as tough as me? Mmm, that I doubt.

To conjure words from the ether. To lay them down in the right order. To ensure they are original. That they make sense. The constant worry that what you are writing down might be gobbledy-gook. It's a huge weight we bear on our shoulders. It's a measure of how stressful our job is that a lot of us writers have a stress ball on our desk. I've had mine for years. I prod it when I'm looking for an adjective. In my darker times I have been known to squeeze it so hard that whatever gloop is contained within has dripped onto my parchment. When I have a deadline, I draw out my craft knife and I stab the stress ball with one hand whilst I type frantically with the other. Show me the equivalent of that sorry little tale within the fire-fighting world. In truth, you won't be able to.

Not that I am complaining. I wouldn't have it any other way. I am happy to be a poet. I know that in spite of the difficulties, in spite of the bruises, the sorrow, if I was to jettison this life and set out on a different calling I would fall at the first hurdle. I wouldn't last five minutes in a bakery, an aquarium, a war zone, a circus or any other workplace you care to throw into the hat. Because I am a poet. For all the horseshit that comes with it, that is the truth of it and something which I cannot, will not, deny. I am a poet, and a bloody important one. And I know I must plough on. And hope that at some stage it monetises.

INTRODUCTION

I f you've ever put together an anthology of *your* poems, you'll know that one of the main things that comes up in meetings and emails is this phrase: 'Which poems will go into the anthology, anyway?'

That was certainly my experience. From the outset there were long discussions as to which of my poems should go into this book. And, more sadly, which shouldn't.

I should clarify, nice and early, that the problem with me has never been that it is difficult to scratch together 'enough' poems. No, quite the reverse. When it comes to quantity, I have an embarrassment of riches. In fact, I've heard it argued that I do better for quantity than I do for quality. Who knows? May be a grain of truth in that. I think there's a debate to be had, though. One thing that is beyond question is this: I've got over 2,000 of the sods. And in other news, I've never had any complaints about the quality of any of them.

So where do you start? I remember at the first full English breakfast I had with Nick – the editor of the original hardback, way back in 2011 – he arrived armed with a wad of my poems. I remember him dealing them onto the table and saying words to the effect of 'These: I like.' I was piercing my fried egg with the corner of my fried bread at the time and barely concentrating on his activities, but that I do remember. These poems spread across the red and white chequered tablecloth, Nick prodding them with a teaspoon. One after another he would poke one and say, 'This one: I like.' I remember sipping my Fanta and thinking, 'So what? Me too.'

The hammer blow came a couple of minutes later when he finished his prodding. He shuffled the poems back up into a wad again and bunged them down next to my bowl of beans. There must have been about thirty of the bastards. 'The question is,' he said earnestly, 'where are we getting the rest from?' I remember nodding as I folded some bread and butter round a hash brown and spooned on some juice that had apparently sweated out of the mushrooms. I remember smiling, too, and leaning right across our plates, right into his face. 'From the same Word document you printed these out from, matey,' I said. And I slotted the hash into my mouth and I leant way back in my chair.

He seemed like he wanted to be the next person to speak, but I held a sausage up to his mouth to shush him. 'I'll just choose the best three hundred,' I continued. He started his next sentence with 'But in terms of quality . . .', but I shut him off; changed the subject to a discussion of where he thought the waiter was from. Nick was silent for a spell, but then adapted to our new topic, suggested maybe Scotland. And the question of 'which poems' remained in my court for the remainder of our relationship.

When I got home I started to pore through my poems. It's difficult to select three hundred poems when you have such an intimidating stack. I know it's a cliché, but they are all my babies. I write them all. I know that sounds unbelievable when you consider the standard and wealth of them, but it's true. Of course I've considered farming them out. Hiring some whizz kid PA to squat at my desk, rattling them off from dawn till dusk, but that's just not how this game works. Ask any poet and they'll tell you the same thing: it's important you have a stake in all your poems. A feeling of ownership. So I write them. And I become very attached to them. And so to just cast a thousand, fifteen hundred, more to one side – well, it's tough. But that was the task, and so I necked maybe a quart of gin and I started hurling clumps of my poems over my head. Huge fistfuls of the sods.

It's tough seeing them go, of course it is. Each poem takes time to conceive, to develop. I nurture them from acorn to oak, each and every one of them. I've got a whole chapter about the grim realities of drafting and redrafting the little urchins in this very book. If you think a poem can just be 'spunked out', or whatever the phrase it is you're using, then you're living in cloud cuckoo land, you really are. I happen to have an enormous amount of respect for my readership and I know that *they* know the difference between a poem that's been dashed off in a second and one that's had a few weeks of care and attention lavished upon it.

And so I just shut my eyes and flung out as many as I could bear. Carnage.

Those that were left I unfolded, ironed, stuck together into sheets, scanned and emailed to Nick. And it is those three hundred that make up this book. Three hundred out of two thousand. The cream. Or, more accurately, some of the cream. Dunked into chapters and positioned pleasingly on the page. They are just the tip, of course, of my poetry iceberg. But though I've sacrificed many in the purge, still enough remain. Or as Nick used to say, sometimes smiling, other times quite solemnly: 'More than enough.'

INTRODUCTION

When the green light flashed go and my dream of cranking out a paperback became reality, I became aware of a certain *major* opportunity. Namely, if they were going to slide this thing through the printing presses again, surely there must be a chance I could slide an extra poem through with it.

I phoned my paperback publisher, Jenny, and asked her about this possibility. Jenny's one of these people who instinctively knows how to deal with people like me. She listened to my idea and then I could hear her clicking the nib of her biro in and out and leafing through the hardback version of the book. She called my idea 'interesting', which was a boost. Then she asked whether I had more poems ready to go. 'Just the two thousand,' came my reply. 'And are they like these ones?' she asked. I said that they were and she was quiet for a bit. 'You betcha they're like those ones,' I reiterated and she said either 'mmm' or 'uh huh'. I can't remember exactly which. Then there was another long silence. She was playing me like a fiddle, is what she was doing. 'I mean, there's a lot of poems in here already,' she said and I said, 'Thank you.' I could hear the nib clicking in and out again. I could hear her whispering my idea to colleagues. I could hear them laughing. They, at least, were on board. 'Just one?' she asked and I made it clear that more than one would be easy, I had oodles – in fact, she was more than welcome to name her figure. 'Just one,' she said again, this time not as a question.

I was excited that Jenny had waved the idea through. I was now at liberty to rifle through all of my poems and choose one that I thought my fan base would appreciate seeing in black and white. My immediate attention turned to the poems I had written in between the hardback hitting the shelves and now: the advent of the paperback. I thought the poem I chose should be a fresh one. One that hadn't been seen before. Like virgin snow, one that hadn't had some great idiot's welly stuck in it. Pristine, untouched. I plunged my huge nose into my sack of poems and started churning through all the ones I'd written in the past three years.

My God, they were good. Just to give you an idea of the standard, here are a couple that didn't get the gig in the end:

POEM#1627
'DOUSING'

Roy fixed a hose to his bell-end.

He roamed around looking for small fires.

And he put them out by pissing through his hose or draping his
     cloak over them.

POEM#2050
'THE TATTOO'

Derreck got a tattoo done.

It said 'I never think about Jessica any more'.

He showed it to his wife.

She asked him why he was getting tattoos done about Jessica.

'Read the tattoo, love!'

Derreck yelled.

'It says I *don't* think about her! That's the point I'm trying to
  make! I *don't* think about her.'

Also, I really liked this one. I liked the idea of having David Platt
somewhere in the book anyway. His swivelled volley in the last
minute against Belgium at Italia 90 is the most beautiful thing I've
ever seen.

POEM#1986
'REEDUCATION'

David Platt had an idea.

He'd take a GCSE.

He got all the forms and tried to enrol.

But my God was it hard!

At night he would go to bed and have nightmares about these
  bloody application forms.

His wife held him.

'You'll be fine, Dave – you'll fill out the forms – I'll help you fill 'em
  out.'

Platt swallowed and clung to her flanks.

He loved his wife.

She made everything okay.

I sent my ideas to Jenny and followed up with a couple of phone
calls and then another email and an email to a colleague of Jenny's

who I knew for a fact sat somewhere near Jenny's desk. I was interested to know whether she felt these were the kind of poems that might capture people's imaginations. The kind that would push the book further into the public's consciousness. When the reply

did come it was far from negative about the poems that I'd proposed. In fact she barely talked about those; more she expressed reservations about the idea of adding a poem, as a whole. Now that she'd thought about it some more, she wasn't sure that there would be space in the newly configured paperback. Also, she wasn't sure that people would necessarily have the appetite for another poem.

I explained that we could make space; if we told the chaps reconfiguring the material they could accommodate another ode, one way or t'other. I heard her nib going in and out like the clappers. I said that if we're making space for seven introductions then I'm sure we can find space for one lousy poem. She asked me what I meant about the seven introductions; I explained my plan to write seven new introductions. More nib action. Then a sigh, then a 'very well', and then my snout back in my sack of poems. I wanted to find a real humdinger for her.

I left no stone unturned. I charged through my back catalogue like a man possessed, reading, chuckling, applauding. Sometimes I would fire one into the ether, to see who saluted. I'd chuck one out of my window, recite one to the Turkish girls who run the dry cleaner's, photograph one and send it to other poets. Anything to make sure I made *the right choice*. The idea of adding one more poem to this anthology and it not being up to snuff made me want to chunder. And the closer I got to choosing one, the more sick I became. Several times I attached a poem to an email to Jenny and then backed out at the last minute, vomiting. No! Not that one! Back into the sack.

And then I found it. The perfect candidate. Beautiful, thought-provoking in every way: sublime. I sent it to Jenny. She wrote back some time later saying 'okay', and it was done.

It's in. It's on page 245. Just nestling there, happy as a clam. In a way it needs no introduction. If I wasn't writing seven, I imagine it wouldn't get one. It's just a simple tale of a man, a bed and, well, who knows. Of course I'm a gibbering wreck this end, worrying it's going to stick out because my style has developed in the years between book formats. I've done a lot of growing up since the hardback. But still. I've been assured, in a separate email from Jenny, that there's no difference in style or – crucially – quality between this poem and the pre-existing material. That's good enough for me. I hope you enjoy the poem. Please, please don't flick forward to it now – find it when you find it – but when you do, please take it in the spirit it is meant. It's a bonus, is what it is. I hope you enjoy it.

INTRODUCTION

Am I a poet? It's a question I have often been *forced into* pondering. I don't want to be pondering it. I don't like pondering it. For me, it's a no-brainer. I am a poet. And yet the insinuations persist. The innuendo. *Other people* raising the question. Making it an issue. And so I have to ponder it. And I get fed up with it.

I don't know why I'm asked it, I really don't. I doubt the other *great poets* ever had to put up with that kind of bullshit question. The Keatses, you know. Plath. These people would never have had some sad little no-mark come up to them, a sloppy old grin plastered all over their face and ask them, 'Would you honestly call yourself a poet?' I doubt Auden would ever have had that. Wordsworth. And yet, honestly, I have to say I'm fielding that question between two and five times a week. Would Pushkin have had that? Is it a factor for McGough?

My response is always dignified.

I've got class. I just haul my hardback anthology from my rucksack and I jab my thumb against the cover. 'Yes, mate!' I'll say. 'Hence why I've got a goddamn anthology!' and I'll open the sod up and I'll leaf through, slapping my palm on top of the poems and saying: 'Is that a poem?' and 'And that one? Feels like that's a poem,' and 'What's that if it's not a poem?' Usually, the chump who's driven me to this comes back with fairly solid answers to these questions, at which point I draw out my iPhone. I find my Wikipedia page and use my thumb and index finger to zone in on the crucial words. 'Tim Key is a poet' it says. And I read it out again and again at these helmets. 'Tim Key is a poet! Say it!' and by the time I'm trudging off, they're saying it back to me, and as I get further away they're corrupting it and saying other things. Variations on a theme. And I jam my fingers in my ears because I don't want to hear it. Any of it.

Evidently the splodges of writing set on the pages of this book are poems. That much is clear. Indeed, revisiting this book, I saw an opportunity to rectify something that's been bugging me for a while. In the hardback version I noticed that every poem was introduced by its title, its number and the word 'poem'. Increasingly I would look at this word and think, 'Well, that's totally unnecessary; of course it's a poem.' You wouldn't visit a gallery and see the word 'art' scrawled above all the lovely paintings. So why must my book be riddled with this word 'poem'? I emailed Jenny about this. I told her the only reason we should be writing 'poem' in this manner is if we consider there's some doubt as to what the fuck these things are. She agreed that that would be the only reason. I emailed again and she told me not to worry about it. I emailed saying I wasn't worried but I'd noticed none of the other poets had the word 'poem' above their poems in their anthologies. She emailed back saying she'd make a call on it. Should think so, too. I look like a bloody idiot with the word 'poem' written above my poems.

Of course, if I'm not a poet there's a problem. A big problem. I've spent my life thinking I am one, so if the rug gets pulled now, what do I have? If I'm not a poet all that's left is for me to reflect on the hours, the days, the weeks, the months, the years, the decades, the God-knows-what, that I've wasted. All that time glugging the sherry, scratching the parchment: to find out it was for nothing would kill me. These must be poems or otherwise nothing makes sense any more. If they're not poems then what the hell was I doing all that time? It would be like someone going up to an acclaimed plumber and saying, 'None of that was plumbing.' His world would fall apart, poor thing. If someone's telling him that 'All that stuff you've been doing under sinks over the years, that's just been basically moving pipes about – you haven't been plumbing.' It would kill him. In fact, the most likely outcome would be that he would fight back. He'd say, 'What? No, I am a plumber. Look, here's my card.' And that's more or less where I am with it. Am I a poet? Yes, here's my card (my card says 'Tim Key: Poet').

So I am a poet then. A professional poet. Published. I'm tempted to say, 'Don't take my word for it – read this book and make up your own mind.' But I think it's that kind of bombastic statement that's caused a lot of the problems. I think better to just say: 'I am a poet – take my word for it.'

INTRODUCTION

I sometimes wonder why I've bothered doing this. I really do. I wonder why I have bothered sacrificing the best part of a decade to write a book. I wonder why the hell I've done that. I wonder what the Dickens I was thinking. I wonder what the fuck I was playing at.

Obviously, I know that's not what you want to hear.

I'm the author, so you're keen to hear news that I'm in control. You want my vibe to be 'I've written a book, I'm happy with it, tuck in.' That's what you'll often see from contemporary authors these days. Go to a book launch, or run into a contemporary author in a café or at a barbecue, and they can generally be found strumming their book smugly against their thigh, purring about its quality. Sometimes they'll find a makeshift stage at whatever social engagement they happen to be at. They'll stand on a table or a climbing frame and waggle their book above their heads and say, 'Yo, arseholes! Check it out!', or words to that effect, and they'll swing their book about like it's their testicles. They're proud of their efforts, a lot of these contemporary authors, and fair play to them.

It's not like I don't like my book. I do. As you start leafing through it, you'll realise it's hard not to love. I just wonder whether I should have plunged ten years into it, that's more the issue. And not just any ten years either. Nope. My thirties. In my darker moments I find it hard to look at that sacrifice, the decade that I have surrendered to this book, without thinking words to the effect of 'Now why have I done that, then?' I look back at all the invitations I declined, the possibilities that I passed by, the moments of joy that I traded in for this book. I wonder what else I might have done had I freed up the space that writing this son-of-a-bitch took up. I once turned down the chance to go on a two-day Danish cookery course. Was it worth it?

I'm sat next to it now. My fat arse is splayed onto a sofa and next to me, scuffed up and riddled with red ink, is my manuscript. Its corners are curled up and it's held in one piece by two huge staples. They are giant, these staples. Proper beasts. At times I can't look at my manuscript. I bite my lip and wince at my own feet; close my eyes altogether, imagine a sporting contest I've watched in the past. Anything not to contemplate the manuscript. At other times I want to pick it up and smother it with kisses. It is Love/Hate. 'Why did I waste my time with you?' yields to 'I will never let you go' as I rifle through her pages, trace my fingers round the poems, squint at the footnotes. And then I sling it down again, go and fix myself a Ribena, put some beans on the hob, phone one of the contacts in my iPhone. Weep into my iPhone. My relationship with my anthology is a complex one.

My darkest moments come when I imagine what else I *could have achieved* in the time I devoted to writing this. If I hadn't wasted my time jizzing this out, what might I have accomplished? This question absolutely pickles me. Obviously the elephant in the room is that I could have become a dentist. Ten years is a *very long time* – I could have started *and finished* my dentistry odyssey in that period. I could have trained for five years, had three very happy years as a qualified dentist, spent a year wondering whether dentistry was definitely for me, jacked dentistry in, gone travelling for a bit, and then started on something else. Ten years! I could have built an eco-home! I could have started a small company renting out lights and other bits and pieces to theatres. I could have had two wonderful marriages. Anything.

And yet for ten years I nurtured this. Like an emperor penguin, I sat on this and did nothing else. I was responsible for this egg. This book. This very tome, which you are now clutching, rested on my penguin feet, my body heat incubating it for a decade.

So I don't know really. I suppose now the ball is in your court. The only way for me to make sense of that decade would be for people like *you* to actually *like the book*. It's perfectly possible. I can name ten people who I know for a fact have liked it. There's my literary agent, Robert, of course. Then there's my mother; she's always tried to be supportive of it. I once had a fan contact me via social media saying that he thought it was fine. When I've asked people outright whether they think it's any good they've nine times out of ten tried to be enthusiastic. I once asked a lover, having encouraged her to read it for several minutes, whether she rated it. She put the book down and very gently pressed her hand against my wrist. I took that as a ringing endorsement.

So go ahead. Fill your fat face with my poems. Eat heartily. I've sacrificed some pretty meaty relationships and a potential career as a dentist getting this piece of shit up and running. Like it. Really, really do your best to *like it*.

SOCIOPOETRY

I have chosen to start my book with this, most relevant of themes. Sociopoetry. Sociopoetry has always fascinated me. In case you are ignorant I will briefly describe the concept of sociopoetry. It is – as you might expect – poetry, which concerns itself with socio. Things falling under the banner of socio would include guns and prisons, the state of hospitals, how much we should give to beggars, whether we should experiment on beggars/force them to become soldiers, her nibs the Queen, the plight of the ethnic and whether there should be a National Lottery – and, if there is, should it be easier to win. My father is a member of society so I have recently been bending his ear about what it is all about. I'll drive to his boathouse and we'll sit down, open a crate of Adnams and try and get to the bottom of things. He has some pretty extremist views, which only begin to make sense after about four Adnams. He believes that single people should be made to ring a heavy, town-crier-style bell when they walk into pubs and multi-millionaires should be forced to carry their first million with them in a large Karrimor rucksack at all times. In addition he doesn't agree with hoodies and he is unsettled by sign language. He thinks that a lot of the ills in society can be traced back to the fact that everyone wears jeans these days. He refuses to even use the word – calling them 'blue trousers' – and can quote some amazing statistics about convicted murderers since the turn of the twentieth century and the colour of their trousers. In addition, he thinks that it would be good to have a president in charge of the whole world (he suggested Michel Platini), he thinks that rock should be easier to buy outside of seaside towns and he believes that he himself should be knighted.

2 I enjoy having these discussions with my (bearded) old man. Once we're good and stoked, and we've put the world to rights, he'll sling his bottle against the wall, trudge over to the rowing machine, take off his blazer and slacks and get down to business. There's no finer sight in sport than my old man, lashed off his skull, a blur of black swimming trunks and white vest, making that flywheel squeal. If I've got half of his appetite for giving a rowing machine a good seeing to when I hit his age I'll be delighted. In truth, I'll be delighted if I'm able to put away the amount of Adnams my old man does at that age, and discuss elements of socio the way he can. He is a very great man.

POEM#714
'THE JOHNNY'

Chris darned his condom in front
   of his electric fire.
Then he slung it in the tin,
Popped it closed
And set off for Clara's.

'BATESY'S BANTER'

4   'While you're down there . . .'
Mike Bates said to Candy.
He'd vaguely thought people would laugh at this.
Unfortunately, the reason Candy was crouching
   near his groin was precisely to pick up a glass
   which Mike had broken.
And also she was his daughter-in-law.
So it didn't get a laugh at all.

'AM DRAM'

Maria sat sobbing in her cell at the   **5**
    all-women's prison.
Why had she stabbed the old man from her
    drama club in Leicester?
And why wouldn't the prison governess let
    her put on *Shakers* by John Godber?

'PR'

6   The Queen took a normal job so the public would
       hate her less.

She became a lollipop lady.

Some hoodlums soon found out about this.

They started goading her; calling her posh and
       firing ducklings at her through a homemade
       bazooka made out of catering-size cans of beans
       fastened together with gaffer tape.

It started to get to Her Majesty.

She would get home, throw her lollipop stick onto
       the couch and be a right cow to the D. of E.

He'd say things like, 'If you don't tell me what's
       wrong I can't help.'

She'd just fart and eat her crisps and carry on
       watching *The Apprentice*.

POEM#1004
'ARNOLD'

Arnold was constantly unhappy **7**

Because he was a maggot (the type of worm).
He knew he couldn't do anything about it.
That he should just get on with it.
But he couldn't help himself.
And so he dwelled on it.[2]

◇◇◇

[2] I expect this is also how people with glasses must feel.

'DERRECK WOODS'

8   Derreck dangled by the dunk-pot.

He caught me staring at his penis.

I quickly averted my stare and pretended

    I was interested in his hip.

And then I loped, awestruck, towards

    the Jacuzzi.[3]

---

[3] This is based on bitter experience. There's a man at my gym without even the vaguest grasp on what it is to be English. After he's showered he just stands there for ages with his dick out. It's as if he finds the idea of covering himself up deeply offensive. I'm only human – I don't go out of my way to look at him but there's only so much of this a man can take before he gets sucked in. Even once he chooses to get dressed, his approach is quite remarkable. Whilst most normal Englishman will start with his grunds and work outwards, this creature opens with the socks and then moves on to his shirt. He's still swinging merrily as he puts his dog collar and crucifix on. There was an occasion last summer where he must have been going straight to a barbecue and actually had his deck shoes on and his rucksack over his shoulder before he put his pants and Bermuda shorts on. I hated this and was physically sick.

POEM#1177
'LOVELY STUFF'

A website was developed.

Homeless guys and people who had mansions
  they weren't using were hooked up.

Suddenly tramps were living in luxury.

They were exultant!

Some of them had staff!

POEM#112
'SIGHTS'[4]

10   I just found out
Someone's trying to kill me!
It's exciting, yes.
But also dangerous.
He's a professional.

◇◇◇

[4] The film *Leon* is superb. It's all about a trained killer who makes friends with a little girl and a plant. He is a Frenchman but you can't help but warm to him in spite of this and the fact that he carves out a living by shooting people dead. One Christmas my brother bought the DVD for his wife but the DVD wasn't in the case. She was furious, but ultimately calmed down and had three beautiful children by him.

POEM#1070

UNTITLED

'Can I have one more crumb please?'
Said the boy from the novel.
'No,'
Said the mean character.
Then the author described the dreadful carpets
    and said how cold it was.

'THE CRUCIBLE'[5]

12   Neil Robertson (the snooker player)
Made eyes at Michaela Tabb
    (the handsome referee).
Ultimately he lost patience and groped her.
She resisted his advances, fending him off
    with a rest.
He sloped back to his chair and started chugging
    down Highland Spring like it was going out
    of fashion.
She tucked her blouse back into her skirt
And awarded Graham Dott the frame.

◇◇◇

[5] I was chasing a girl and got us tickets to watch John Higgins vs Anthony Hamilton at the Crucible in 1997. Our tickets were for the evening session and Higgins had won the match in the afternoon with a session to spare so it was a bit of a letdown. In the end they wheeled out Willie Thorne and Dennis Taylor to do trick shots and tell anecdotes about their time in snooker so they wouldn't have to give refunds to us punters. It was all right. Willie Thorne used George Best's line about spending ninety per cent of his money on women and drink and wasting the rest. That went down pretty well. Lottie didn't know what to make of it. Watching these old-timers egging each other on and me in her ear making excuses for them. On the way home she was loath to speak to me. She said that she felt betrayed; that she was too nice a girl to be treated like this. She was walking quickly, clutching her programme to her chest in the drizzle. I could barely keep up. I kept on yelling after her that I hadn't planned on

UNTITLED

'What am I doing here?'

This was Margaret Lowe.

'We're imprisoning you.'

This was the captain.

'Please move your hand so I can shut the
    cell door.'

This was the captain's assistant.

---

watching those guys. I kept on shouting 'I'm not a sicko!' She wouldn't
listen though. 'The tickets were for John Higgins!' I kept yelling. By this
stage I was on my knees and it was raining hard.

'PUBLIC REACTION'

14   A pop star changed her hairstyle.
      And everyone hated it.
      Literally every single person in the country (UK)
      Absolutely hated it.
      It was long at the sides and on the top and short
          at the front and back.
      But – to reiterate – *everyone hated it.*
      In fact, when she came out and did her first song
          literally every single person in the O2 arena
          whistled and threw shit at this pop star.
      She got them back on side by singing a couple
          of classics.
      But then everyone remembered her hair and,
          ultimately, she was lynched and eaten.

POEM#994
'SUSPICION'

Michael put 50p in his piggy bank every day
   for three years.
He smashed it open.
There was two pound fifty in there.
He frowned and looked up at his cellmate.

'WRENCHED'[6]

◇◇

[6] In the end a decision was made not to print this one. It was decided that it was sexist and that, in the current climate, there's no sense in *seeking out* controversy. If you're good enough it will come to you. It was frustrating for me because, as I kept arguing with my editor, I don't think the lass in the poem is particularly degraded. Or at least you can argue that some girls would, actually, be pretty happy to get involved with this sort of thing. My editor suggested that the feminists might not see it like that and I responded that, frankly, I couldn't give too much of a shit about those guys. Truth be told, I've not got a great deal of time for feminism, and this in spite of the fact that, purely in terms of lineage, I am myself half female. In 2008 I was invited to do a recital at a conference about feminism in London and the whole experience left a sour taste. During a break between seminars I went for a dump in the ladies'. They didn't like that much. They were throwing perfume bottles into my cubicle, calling me every name under the sun. I was just standing there with my trousers round my ankles, yelling that I thought they were crazy. I said I was breaking down barriers and reasoned that they should be applauding me – not attacking me. One of them threw a Kenwood mixer over the door. I continued to claim, as articulately as I could, that they were only feminist when it suited them.

POEM#520

'PLANS'

Shawn watched the two black belts[7]
   demonstrating.
He frowned.
It would take him ages to get that bloody good.
Then he smiled.
But once he was . . .
Well – Benjamin, Glass Derreck and the other
   one wouldn't know what had hit 'em.

◇◇

[7] I tried karate once. I was living in Russia and putting on weight because of their food and culture. A friend was joining a karate class so I went along out of interest. I couldn't understand the instructions per se so I was drawing a lot on my recollections of kung fu films and those guys you'd sometimes get on *Record Breakers* who karate-chopped a pile of bricks to impress Roy Castle. I went to two classes but I found that the inside of my elbow hurt so I quit. On Saturdays we used to go on walks with a Russian family someone had found on the Tube. One time they invited us to their home for tea. They had nothing and yet gave everything. It was very humbling. After tea we watched *Octopussy* in Russian. I wasn't full but I didn't say anything because I was still feeling humbled. When we left we bought ice cream from an invalid. That stuff tasted *too good*.

WAR AND PEACE AND RELIGION AND SHOPPING

Love it or loathe it, we all have an opinion on war. Funny to think that, generations ago, people were tumbling over the dunes with their archaic guns and blowing up Nazis with a view to *ending war altogether*. Of course, as time has gone on we find that the odd war does no real harm and, in fact, is good for things like technology, tourism and the nation's sense of self worth. One thing's for sure, I couldn't do it myself. I'd enjoy the travelling side of it, of course, but I'd hate the other, well documented, downsides. For me the opening half hour of *Schindler's List* provokes the same reaction as an episode of *The Office* – I'm behind the sofa, cringing; I can barely watch. The idea of staggering around on a beach looking for my own arm fills me with dread, quite honestly. Also, I am one of these people who overthinks things, so, even though I'd know, deep down, that I was being daft, I'd be worrying that a lot of the soldiers I was peppering with bullets might be really great guys. Of course, there's no way of checking this, as, by the time you're close enough to chat to them, or to see if there is common ground in terms of tastes in music et cetera, the evil buggers have peeled off a dozen pellets into your eye. I have talked to my father about this. He openly admits he took the coward's way out and was born *right at the very end* of WWII. He has no great lust for war and, in his darker moments, has stated that he thinks there should be no more wars at all. The money saved, he argues, could be plunged into more sophisticated paintballing centres to satiate the needs of the bloodthirsty. On several occasions I have stated to him that without wars a large part of my income, of any poet's income, would be hugely compromised. At this point he starts spouting nonsense like 'Why can't you write about peace?' and we have to agree to disagree. To write poems where no one is suddenly obliterated by a bomb would be overwhelmingly disrespectful to the likes of Wilfred Owen, Siegfried Sassoon and those other brave balladeers who risked all to report on death for our entertainment. And so it is that I have devoted a whole section to war (with a couple of poems about religion and some shopping ones thrown in so we don't slit our wrists at the horror of it all!).

POEM#681
'THE RULES OF WAR'

Lee snuck off to get a crêpe and some beer.
When he came back to the trench his major gave
   him a right ticking off, including killing him
   with his revolver.

'THE REALITIES OF WAR'

22 Oliver Hampton-Church,
    Whose main trick was to pretend he was
        surrendering and then shoot Germans
        through his flag,
    Eventually shot so many holes through it that it
        stopped covering up his gun enough, and a
        Japanese chap cut his head off.[8]

---

[8] The war poetry I include is not, then, based on my own experience. It is based on the experience I imagine the poor buggers on the front line have to go through. I tend to go to Dunkirk or Calais or at the very least Dover if I'm going to write war poetry. Last summer I went there with some lads. We did the hypermarkets and then cruised the museums. I snuck off a couple of times and scribbled down a few ideas and then we'd meet up and grab some food in the evening. On our last night we split up and all went to different restaurants and then reconvened in a tavern by the front. One of the lads was still hungry and it later transpired that he hadn't gone to a restaurant at all. He had walked out across the sands and dipped his head into the edge of the ocean.

POEM#679

'THE AWKWARDNESS OF WAR'

Matt was literally all over the place.

A bomb had banged near him and three
    chunks had hit him.

The worst one was about as big as a hubcap
    (if the car was as big as a Labrador).

It went *woomph* into his chin and he went woozy
    straight away.

He couldn't see shit.

'Horace! Horace!'

He yelled at the soldier next to him.

But things went from bad to worse.

Embarrassingly, it wasn't Horace but a different
    man from another regiment.

Matt cringed and pretended he was calling past
    this ginger guy to an imagined Horace a little
    further towards the sea –

And safety.

POEM#329

UNTITLED

24 A Christian[9]

Noticed he was good at sprinting.

He arranged a 100 metre fun run for

his congregation.

Not only did he finish a disappointing fifth,

But his vicar beat him wearing a gown and

cassocks and clutching an orb.

◇◇◇

[9] People often forget that this section is partly devoted to Religion. Far be it from me to pontificate about Religion. So much has been said about the existence or otherwise of Christians, you hardly need me to wade in with a well-meaning effort to 'settle it once and for all'. We're all old enough and daft enough to make up our own minds by now, I think. Suffice to say that a man in whom I trust completely (Rick) reckons he's been inside a Church, and I've seen videos he's taken on a camera phone of a vicar, which seem genuine. But then if you look at the chaps abroad who are promoting their Korans and blowing their chests up – they swear blind that the whole thing is much more to do with mosques and synagogues. Very thorny thing, Religion. For what it's worth, I think there must be something in it, or how do you explain the endless bloodshed?

POEM#1101
'THE INCIDENT IN RYMAN'S'

Chris hadn't seen Tania for about three years
    when they bumped into each other in
    Ryman's and he forgot her name.
This was very embarrassing, to say the least.
But, typically, Chris talked his way out
    of trouble.
And soon he was fucking her against a fax
    machine that also photocopied.

'SHOPPING GARRETT'

26 Lesley Garrett[10] frowned.

Her fist was bleeding.

'I'm afraid we simply don't recognise that

as a method of payment,' the sales

assistant repeated.

'But it's worth more than that telly!' Garrett

yelled; and she punched the bit on the

till again.

The bald sales assistant went deeply ashen.

'You can't pay by singing,'

He reiterated.

But Garrett had already slotted her backing CD

into a nearby Denon.

She waded back to the till, ordered a weak boy to

bag up her widescreen, spat out her gum and

began to sing.

◇◇

[10] I had a big row with one of the builders about this lady. I mentioned that I'd watched a television show called *Who Do You Think You Are?: With Lesley Garrett*. He corrected me and said the show was called *Who Does Lesley Garrett Think She Is?* I told him he'd got that one wrong – I argued that this was just an angry thought he'd had in his head. He kept on shouting details from the show out to prove he'd seen it. He was brandishing a large tool that looked like it was designed to tighten things but also had a blade on it, and yelling things like 'HER GREAT

'THE FUTILITY OF WAR'

All the soldiers were on the beach throwing
    bombs at each other.
After two hours Alan hit a horrid German and
    that meant they'd both lost exactly 300
    sons/people.
Richard giggled.
'We're back where we started.'
Then an accurate German fired a bullet
    through his neck, and that was him
    done, too.

◇◇

GRANDFATHER SOLD PIANOS', so eventually I had to back down and
he called me a pussy – and continued to call me that, in fact, whilst I made
him a cup of tea.

POEM#838
'THE FURIOUS CITIZEN'

28   Philip dropped a bomb from his plane onto
        some foreign soldiers.
    Everyone who knew someone who died was
        very upset.
    One woman actually shook her fist at
        Philip's plane.

'THE SIKH AND THE CHRISTIAN'

A Sikh and a Christian[11]

Traded religions

For the rest of the day

The Sikh died that afternoon – an enormous
    icicle fell through him.

The Christian – as a tribute – stayed Sikh for
    a further month.

◇◇

[11] It's always heartening to see people from two religions playing nicely together. It tends to work best with things like babies and little boys and girls, as they haven't been taught who to discount yet owing to their beliefs. I read an account once (possibly apocryphal) about a Buddhist gentleman who lent a Christian his lawnmower. When you hear stuff like that you can't help but remain hopeful, exultant even. I remember when I read that article I dashed straight down to the shops and had a couple of cans of Guinness to celebrate. I then scanned the article and sent it out to the guys to see what they made of it. They loved it and I got them over to my gaff and cooked for them. Most of them were already lashed by the time they arrived. One of them brought an American girl.

'CORPORAL MOORE'S MISSION'

30   Corporal Moore
      Was asked to go undercover.
      He would be shot, pierce enemy lines as a ghost
      And – hopefully –
      Report back to Sergeant Cornwall (a medium).

POEM#1183
'THE END'

The penises in charge of the world
Set off two whopping great nuclear bombs –
One going in each direction.
Everyone died, including the guys who had
    organised the bombs.
There was a pretty depressing silence.
Some Eskimos survived because they were
    wrapped in thick coats made out of seal
    blubber and penguin fur.
They continued to bore holes in the ice and
    pull fish from the ocean to eat.

POEM #335
'PRAYER'

32   Jack Manchester went to church 100 times.

He got brilliant at praying.

One day he prayed that Denise would sit on
    the same pew as him.

She did, and he allowed himself the luxury of
    touching her knee with his wrist.

POEM#922
'INVESTMENT'

Abigail spent twelve grand on a haircut.[12]
In fairness to Abigail, it suited her and she
　　pulled a Premiership footballer.

---

[12] I wasn't sure whether this poem should go in this section. It's in on a technicality. The technicality being that, on balance, I think you can classify getting a haircut as shopping. There's a fine line and I'm sure I'll be hung out to dry in the press for making this claim. I definitely see that you don't buy a haircut in the same way that you buy carrots or a copy of *Mayfair* or a Bill Bryson book. But I still definitely see it as a purchase. I also see having coffee in Starbucks, enrolling on a kickboxing course or throwing money into a wishing well as shopping.

'THE LOGISTICS OF WAR'

34 China and America both wore blue to the war.
The Chinese were furious.
'Didn't you get our emails!!!?'
The Americans explained that Elaine, the girl
    who dealt with all that side of things, was off
    on maternity leave.
They agreed it was their bad and offered to go
    skins until their away kit could be flown over.
They stripped down to their boots and trousers
    and put their war jackets in the backs of
    their tanks.
Then they poured forward across the deserts,
    shouting their heads off and firing their
    guns and chucking grenades and rocks at
    the Chinese.
The Chinese returned fire,
Warm and smart in their blue fatigues.

'GOD BEING GOD'

God made a cloud in the shape of a famous
    politician taking a shit.
Then he waited for people to notice it,
Trying hard to suppress his giggles.

WOOING, SCREWING AND CHEWING

My father pulled my mum at a fancy dress party. He was dressed up as a schoolmaster and she was there as a pirate. One doesn't like to rake over old ground but I imagine he probably spluttered some bon mot about piracy, got her giggling, engaged her in conversation, discussed his voluntary work as a scout leader and then possibly had her feel his beard. There would have been nothing smutty or improper. Because it was a different era! There then would have followed a respectful period of courting. My father would have bought or stolen flowers for my mother and she would have blushed and entered whichever restaurant or bingo hall my father had opened the door to and ushered her into. He would have been respectful, and ultimately he would marry and sleep with her. My mother. These days such exploits would be unheard of. These days people grab whoever's nearest, get off with them, get their full name for Facebook purposes and hope that warmth and companionship will automatically follow. Young men and women just don't have the patience to wait for a fancy dress party. Their heads have been contaminated by Page 3 and *Skins* and Richard

Keys and pornographic websites, and they roam around in a daze, like zombies, banging into each other, falling on top of each other, humping each other, apologising to each other. It doesn't do to overthink this sort of thing but I imagine part of the problem is the fact that the Church has had a difficult few decades, so they can't make people act the right way like they used to be able to. So you've then got to ask why this has happened. How has the Church lost it? For my money, it's in large part due to the fact that people have begun to find the sermons limited and unexciting, and so they've stopped putting their hands in their pockets during collections and so the Church haven't had the brass to hire the sort of charismatic preachers that they would need in order to compete with more vibrant industries such as TV, sport and cinema. So we are left without any saintly guidance; we are content to chalk up sexual partners like they're going out of fashion. Do we blame Tiger Woods for his dismal conduct? Hang him out to dry in our redtops? Damn him in our poetry anthologies? Or do we blame mean Christians for not putting more coins in the velvet bag? I know one man who's screwed six girls called Claire Smith, and has his eye on a seventh. Thankfully, you do still get exceptions to this morally bankrupt norm. You can still find the odd square waddling up to his date with a bag of posies, pecking her on the cheek and steering her into a community organised dance, but largely things have become much more aggressive, immediate and grubby. Where possible, of course, I make a point of bucking this trend. I am always at pains to be as romantic as the situation allows. Recently, I cooked dinner for a young Spanish lady. She was very appreciative. I was ladling beans and spice-infused cress onto our plates like a man possessed – Norah Jones belting out of my Sony Hi-Fi as God intended. I had lit candles and joss sticks and hollowed out a pumpkin by way of effort and she was glowing in the face of my commitment to romance. It was quite a night! My only complaint was that she insisted on leaving in a taxi prior to pudding. Once she had left, I sat in front of the snooker and, reflecting on my evening, became deeply annoyed. It struck me that, having splashed out on flowers, dinner ingredients and a residential cooking course to get me to a sufficient standard to approximate Spanish cooking, I had in fact spent more than it would have cost me to hire exactly the type of professional sex worker I had been trying to avoid paying. And yet, owing to my old-fashioned, romantic obsessiveness, I didn't even get to experience anything remotely intimate with Martina. Not a handshake, not nothing. In short, it was a fucking washout.

POEM#948
'ONLINE BULLSHIT'

40   Two ugly bastards

Gave false faces to an Internet dating site.

But they got each other.

When they met they were both bloody furious.

POEM#1129

'THE SAD TALE OF CHRIS AND SIAN'

Chris and Sian started having an affair.[13]
But Sian couldn't wink properly.
So everyone found out and they had to end it.

---

[13] I could never have an affair. I am claustrophobic, so can't stand the idea of being trapped naked inside a wardrobe, waiting until my lover has convinced her husband that those are her underpants and those are her cans of Guinness.

POEM#229
'CHARM'

42 My future wife eyeballed me across
    our pancakes.
She was still in her
Waitressing outfit.[14]
I made another joke about that.

---

[14] I don't have a thing about girls in uniforms – which always surprises me.

POEM #1184

'DYING WISHES'

Maurice lost his wife to flu, and, some days later,
    found himself at a speed-dating[15] night.
Over the next 10 weeks he attended 16 sessions
    and chatted to over 170 women.
In the gaps between the sessions he hooked up
    with the women he had met at the sessions and
    he slept with them.
He was bedding two and a half girls a day.
By night he was banging the organizers.
When she had died in his arms, Victoria had told
    him that he must move on,
He must see other women.
This was whence he drew his strength.

〰〰〰〰〰〰〰〰〰〰〰〰〰〰〰〰〰〰〰〰〰〰〰〰〰〰〰〰〰〰〰〰〰〰〰

[15] I've tried speed dating a couple of times. I hate it. All the awkwardness becomes condensed and gets reset every ten minutes. Misery. The only advantage is that none of the girls know how quickly I'm drinking. I went to a speed dating event just outside Warwickshire once. I tipped a barman pretty heavily early in the piece and after that I was scooping up pints between dates with very little fuss. He had my card behind the bar so the process was easy as pie. I was using him a lot like a water-stop in a marathon. After a couple of hours I was all over the place, turning up late to dates, lunging at the participants and organisers. My shirt was untucked and my hair was sticking to my forehead. The only consolation was that in order to get a rounded view of how badly I behaved that evening, the girls would have had to have sat down and pieced it all together. And I know for a fact they didn't do that, as I was the last to leave.

POEM#467

'THE COMPLIMENT'

44   I dated a girl.
She looked a lot like Lee Westwood.
I tried to explain who he was.
'He's a golfer,' I kept on saying.
Karen self-consciously covered her face
     and blubbed through my description
     of Westwood's record in majors.

POEM#149
'THE DATE'

Two lesbians[16]
Turned up for their date
Carrying the same type of flowers.
They got off with each other
And then went to their film.

‹◇◇◇›

[16] I worked with a lesbian for a bit (in the 1990s). She was Czech and was married to a stone mason. We used to take lunch together and, ultimately, we took a trip to the village of her birth – about an hour outside of Prague. Her family's flat was rather Eastern European and you had to go through the bathroom if you wanted to go from the kitchen into the lounge. All this meant is that if you were having a bath someone might walk past you carrying food, so you had to cover your knob with your hands. I loved the bars in this lesbian's village – they served cheap Staropramen and fried cheese, and in one of them a man played a guitar. I was fond of this girl and knew her for a year. In the end, she gave me a book by Bohumil Hrabal before moving, in a very dignified manner, to Salisbury.

'A SAD POEM'

46   Jeff (Jeff Quinn)

Loved Anna.

He did 'daring acts' for Anna.

He rode to Anna's work with no trousers on.

He lit his hair outside Anna's badminton.

He snuck her name into his auction patter.

*

Anna never noticed Jeff (Jeff Quinn).

She was too busy embarking on relations with

    a different auctioneer.

That is – she was screwing Mr Redmond

    (Jim Redmond) every single night

    in his flat.

POEM#982

'TOO MUCH CHEWING GUM IN ONE GO'

Elizabeth

47

Put seventy packets of chewing gum[17] in her
  mouth at once.

It was too much gum.

Her jaws fell off and she died.

---

[17] My father has never chewed gum. He has also never had scampi and he has never ordered anything from the specials board in a restaurant ('If they could cook it, it would be on the main menu *full time*'). One year he bought my mum a stylus for his record player for her birthday. Another year he bought her a car battery. When we were little, he'd take me and my brother to the newsagent's to get a paper and some comics. My brother had a little chair behind the saddle and I'd be stuffed in the basket. These days, when he does any painting around the house he wears brown shorts from the 1970s and a Fred Perry t-shirt, which is also from the 1970s and is also brown, but a very different brown. When he was a teenager, my father smoked a pipe.

POEM#491
'CLIFFORD'S PEN'

48 Clifford bought a pen.[18]

It cost £16.99 but in actual fact it was just
a Bic biro.

He got stick from all the other social workers.

They used phrases like 'they saw you coming'
and 'daylight robbery' and 'you've paid over
the odds'.

But Clifford didn't care.

He liked his new biro – even though he had
to shake it and lick it to make it work.

And he started using his new pen to write his
love letters to Genevieve.

<hr>

[18] When I write I use a Mitsubishi Uniball. They are very smooth and come in a variety of different colours – for example, black. Most days I'll buy a new Mitsubishi Uniball and scribble it dry. If I'm writing something slightly more involved then I will switch up to the Lamy. Lamy is a European company who make all manner of pens. I have a Lamy fountain pen which is claret in colour and goes like a dream. One of the fringe benefits of the Lamy is that it comes in a sheath so the whole thing seems that much more significant. If I were ever to write a letter to Gary Lineker or President Barack Obama, I would use the Lamy. I'd buy a really nice postcard from a gallery, have a couple of glasses of Baileys, slide my Lamy out of its sheath, get my thoughts down and get it posted.

POEM#824
'TYPICAL ERNEST'

Mandy Gandhi –

The naughty Indian girl –

Performed seven wonderful sex acts on Ernest
    and I.

During one of the ones on Ernest, he cried out
    the phrase 'I love you!'

Trust old Ernest to lose his composure.

She just looked at me and winked.

I panicked and blew her a kiss.

'MAUD'

50 John wanted to screw Maud.
    'But Maud wouldn't be interested in that as
        an idea,'
    John thought to himself.
    He wrote her a poem:

    'Maud.
    I'm hoping to strike a chord.
    Could you afford me twenty minutes of your busy schedule?
    To have sex with your landlord.[19]

    When the reply eventually came back, it was
        actually from Maud's grandson on behalf
        of Maud.
    She wanted to know if it would be 'no strings'.

◇◇

[19] This is an example of *a poem within a poem*. I'm not 100 per cent sure anyone else has ever done/would ever dare to do this sort of thing. Of course, Shakespeare could barely help himself having *a play within a play*, but *a poem within a poem*? I doubt it. My mother sometimes serves a meal within a meal. She makes a risotto and pushes it into a ring around the edge of the plate and then throws some fish and chips into the middle of it. My dad loves that sort of thing but she usually only cooks it if she's doing a dinner party. She did it for Wendy and John a while back. They were applauding and banging their cutlery on the table. They'd never seen

POEM#475
'A TOUCHING MOMENT'

Steve West

Touched a breast

And boasted to his mates.

Wendy Carr

Readjusted her bra

And sat herself down on some crates.

anything like it. John was slapping my old man on the back and saying how jealous he was that my old man was married to a creature capable of such wonders. My dad explained that she wouldn't do it *just for him* – that it was just for when folk came round. He looked very wistful.

POEM#811

'A LOADED GUY'

52   I stole £400,000
And then flashed it about, to get an ideal
  girlfriend.
Eventually I lured this greedy
  35-year-old model.
She was the absolute pits –
A demanding beauty, who stayed on the gravy
  train for a good six weeks.
I lavished her with gifts (tiara, gym
  membership, chemise, countless Covent
  Garden soups).
Then all the money went and she faded back
  into obscurity.
And now I'm alone once more.
And planning my next fraud.

POEM#1128
'THE BEGINNING'

Morne needed a pen.[20]

He gestured to the waitress.

She misread his mime and brought him the bill.

They giggled about the misunderstanding and
    later married.

---

[20] If I were ever to write to Gary Lineker, I would probably ask him to give me some anecdotes about getting lashed with Terry Butcher at Italia 90. I'd also get him to dish the dirt on Peter Beardsley and ask him whether using an autocue took a bit of getting used to when he first got the MOTD gig. I'd probably tell him some of my own news, too.

'THE TRAGEDY OF HOPE'

54   Martin Blousy waited under the big clock thing
    in Waterloo Station.
He was clutching a large bouquet of flowers and
    dressed in his best togs – scarlet suit, cravat,
    sandals, beret, bangles et cetera.
The clock read 1.55 p.m.
He was a little early so played Snake and ate
    a Magnum.
He was excited about watching a Russian film
    at the NFT/BFI.
The clock read 2.05 p.m.
Martin blinked and played Snake.
Where was she?
He ate another Magnum.
The clock read 2.20 p.m.
Martin had a snoop around Paperchase and
    fiddled with his bangles.
The clock read 3.15 p.m.
Where was she? Where was Anne? Tut.
The clock read 5pm and a black swan sat on
    it ominously.

Martin caused a diversion and stole a chair from
    Costa Coffee.
He plonked it under the clock and licked his
    latest Magnum.
It was a quarter to eleven, and some drunk
    people kicked him owing to his cravat.
He explained to a guard he was waiting for the
    most beautiful girl he'd ever met – a cross
    between Gabrielle and the female snooker ref,
    Michaela Tabb.
On the second day he ate another half dozen
    Magnums and thought about texting Anne.
'Have a little faith,' he scolded himself.
By October he was starting to seriously doubt
    himself. He was now openly staring at
    the clock.
Brilliantova Ruka had almost certainly finished
    its run.
The winter proved too much for Martin.
    He died on February 6th.
He wrote a note on a card from Paperchase that
    was in the HH price category

(continued)

56   Saying he should not be moved.
Saying he was waiting for someone.
Anne arrived the following August. She looked
     dead guilty as she and her husband laid four
     fresh lilies on Martin's skeleton.
There was a note attached. 'Everything's been
     really hectic recently.'
She kissed a rib and left, bright red
     with embarrassment.

HEROES OF OUR TIME

I love heroes. They are such inspirational, proactive beasts. These men and, usually, women, who just will not stand by and let things take their course. The one man (or, in most cases, woman) in a thousand who will stand up, kick his chair away, throw down his pasty and yell 'NO'. The individuals who think nothing of braking suddenly, leaping from their cars and haring up the embankment – headlong into the danger. The movers and shakers, the law-breakers, the cake-makers. The mavericks, the daredevils, the unhinged bell-ends – that rare breed of gallant pricks who are brave enough to choose their own paths through life, to call their own shots, and the consequences can go hang. Tellingly, I think, when one thinks of heroes, those who come to mind are all too often from the dim and distant past. If I say, 'Name me five heroes!', chances are you'll shoot back something along the lines of 'Robin Hood, Kelly Holmes, Geldof, Jesus and that Dutch cunt who stuffed his finger in the dam'. Heroism was that much more *de rigueur* back in the day. Now that our world is stuffed to the gills with things like Twitter and digital radios and hi-vis cycling bibs, acts of heroism seem somehow out of place. In fact, you could be forgiven for thinking that the only heroes still operating today do so in the murky world of fiction. Superman, the hunky American gentleman in the blue tights and red knickers, is often held up as the very embodiment of heroism. A proud, morally upstanding beefcake, not afraid to get mucked in and burn a criminal's legs with his eyes, or risk getting wet by plunging into the Niagara Falls to save an irritating journo. Here *was* a hero – in some people's eyes, a superhero, even. But even in Superman's case, it was in real life that the most astounding heroics were to be found. Clark Kent, the actor who portrayed Superman, fell off his horse whilst competing in an equestrian event and paralyzed his legs and arms. He was condemned to be plonked in a wheelchair for the rest of his days, but confronted his fate with a determination and courage more than equal to the beleotarded Man of Steel he portrayed on the big screen. Inspired by his wife's strength and support he began to fight and to adapt and to rehabilitate, mining impossible reserves of self-belief from untold depths. Not three years after his horrifying injury, Kent was back on screen in award-winning form in a remake of Hitchcock's *Rear Window*. He also topped the *New York Times* bestseller list; worked tirelessly to promote work on spinal-cord injury; and fought to teach other paralyzed people to live more independently. His tale is inspirational. Some say that *this*, and not *Superman*, is the real Hollywood Story. That Kent's achievements in real life outdid those of his sexy alter ego. A film should be made of Kent's life! Indeed the only thing that would be more remarkable than a film of Kent's life would be if the actor portraying Kent somehow became blessed with the ability to fly across oceans and bend steel with his own hands, in real life. If that happened then they would obviously have to make a movie of *that* actor's life. And then we would be in a loop. We should be truly inspired by Kent's story. However, let us not become awed by it. Because, if you look hard enough, it is possible to unearth tales of heroism closer to home.

They are few and far between, sure. But heroes walk amongst us. My father is a prime example. A normal, bearded man, he has so far organised about twenty fun runs, climbed about a hundred mountains and put away about three hundred banoffee pies. On a day-to-day basis he is either attempting or flat-out *nailing* acts of heroism. One morning he'll be scooping a lame calf out of a weir, the next he'll be clambering up a tree to rescue a child's balloon. On weekends he will take his stepladder, black swimming trunks and referee's whistle down to the river and set himself up as a freelance lifeguard. By night he will scuttle about with his torch and his baton, looking for skirmishes to put an end to. He carries rope with him, always ready to haul the afflicted. Never one to boast about his acts of heroism, he just pops them up on his website, informs the local papers and moves on with a shrug of those broad shoulders. I spoke to him about heroism on one of our recent camping trips. We cooked eggs and rice over an open fire and he drank stout and bitter as he spoke. He said that for him it comes naturally and he doesn't do it for the plaudits. 'Some people are born heroic,' he said, and he stood up to remind me of his build. He looks heroic. As we drank more, he spoke about The State. He wondered whether The State could offer more support for our heroes. Some kind of system could be introduced, he thought – a means of taxing the unheroic in order to make the heroic community a little more comfortable. He said it makes him laugh when people try and divvy the money out 'fairly' so that you end up with unexceptional also-rans having exactly the same benefits and penalties as the real high-fliers. He leaned across the fire and his beard smouldered as he spoke: 'Someone like Ray Mears shouldn't be paying tax,' he said. I couldn't argue with this. 'The guy knows how to hollow out a canoe, for heaven's sake!' He grabbed his knife and started scratching the mechanics of what he proposed onto the stump of a tree. Factory workers, he etched, would pay a penny more in the pound. The money accrued would then be used to ensure that people like Mears and Jamie Oliver and Jane Horrocks and Andy Murray and himself would get to live in luxury. He blew away the excess wooden residue and threw his knife over his shoulder. It impaled a bat against a low bough. I nodded at my father and watched as he clumped towards his hammock. 'Night then,' I said. He was peeling off his Fred Perry, ready for his bed. I smiled. What a man. What a hero.

UNTITLED

I heard tell of a man who has fucked Beyonce,
Won Wimbledon
And scored five A-stars at school.
He also rides his bike no-handed.
And his spaghetti Bolognese is *extraordinary*.
It is humbling to hear his tale.

'SHACKLES'

62 Harold didn't go to work one day.

'Sod work!' he thought.

He got up late, checked his emails, checked
  his MySpace and checked to see if there was
  anything new on Google.

Then he drank coffee and sent a group text,
  bragging, and calling his friends suckers.

In the end he went in just before lunch and
  got an official warning.

But, boy, did he feel alive!

POEM#1151
'THE MAIN ANT'

An ant
Broke all the carrying records.
Just to give an idea,
Most ants can't carry much more than a shit
    piece of leaf.
This cunt could carry a two-litre bottle
    of cider.

'THE GREATER GOOD'

64   Carlo –

The Italian shepherd who sometimes slept with
   his flock –

Became depressed when the droughts came.

He couldn't cope when his sheep went thin.

Ultimately, he sacrificed himself.

He took his own life by knocking himself on his
   head with his crook.

And his flock nourished themselves on his corpse

And they survived until the rains.[21]

◇◇

[21] I am fascinated by tales of heroes perishing for The Greater Good. Overwhelmingly, it happens in films (*Armageddon*), but it has started to cross over into real life. How many times have we read articles in free newspapers or listened to people at dinner parties recalling those articles – grim descriptions of heroes scurrying around in burning houses or beastly warzones, saving others and perishing themselves? You can't help but think what *you* would have done. Would *you* have the stones to take a bullet for a stranger? Would *you* tell someone if they were about to get squashed by a falling phonebox? On these dilemmas I think I'm 50/50, or worse. So whenever I meet anyone who has been courageous enough to give their life in order that their fellow man is spared, I shake them warmly by the hand and tell them, 'Name your drink'. These are valiant folk. Better than us. And should be treated accordingly. 'Name your drink, sir! And would you care for some crisps?'

POEM#935
'DONALD'

Donald
Bought a tent,
And he bought 3,000 cans of Grolsch beers,
And he bought 15 loaves of Hovis,
And he set off for Suffolk
For some Donald time.

'THE WOODEN MAN'

66 Pinocchio[22] –

The wooden chap whose snout grows when he
    speaks shit –

Told thirty lies in a row so that it got to about
    eight foot!

Then he switched the telly on without getting up.

His date, Nicky, was embarrassed and appalled.

---

[22] I hold my hands up – I think this one's in the wrong section. I think I fell into the trap of thinking that Pinocchio is a hero, based on all the propaganda you are fed as a child. In actual fact the guy's full of shit. The goon should be nowhere near a heroes' section – simply because of the tissue of lies he was always peddling. In my opinion, people shouldn't lie unless they absolutely have to (affairs/explaining why you've got drugs at customs). If I ever suspect someone is lying to me, I call them on it immediately. I hate being lied to. I'll sometimes put my forehead right up close to theirs and move them backwards with it so they get scared I'm about to head-butt them. I read those books today and I just shake my head at Geppetto. Of course Pinocchio is arsehole-in-chief here, but Geppetto's such a dopey old sod for not fastening onto him sooner. Clearly the guy's not all the ticket, getting outsmarted by that shit-filled wooden goon. He winds me up, does Geppetto.

POEM#1193
'FOR MY PASSENGERS' SAKE'

There was a gap in the track and the train was
    heading right for it.
The train driver noticed this and hated it.
He threw down his sandwich and sprung
    into action.
He tried to jump out of his cabin and throw
    himself into the gap to act as additional track
    so the train could keep going.
This obviously didn't even come close
    to working;
His back was ripped to shreds and the train
    bounced into a forest.

POEM#863
'BROWN'S EYE'

68   'Which one's the glass one?'
Obama said.
'Huh?'
Brown grunted.
This was all in the Oval Office.
'Which eye's made of glass, man?'
'Oh. This.'
Obama reached a finger into Brown's eye.
His nail tapped the glass orb twice.
Tappety-tap.
There was a magical sound.
Obama smiled.
Brown blinked.
'You've turned it into a real eye,' he said.
'Guilty.' Obama.
'You clever swine.' Brown.
'It's what I do.' Obama.
'I'll take care of all the economics stuff.' Brown.
'Swell.' Obama.
'We'll be unstoppable.' Brown.
And so on.

'THE MODEST MAN WITH THE CRAMPONS'

Clark Watchman

Was an amazing mountaineer.

Seriously – he was really amazing.

But he didn't like to talk about it.

If anyone said so much as, 'I saw you made
   mincemeat out of Mont Blanc last week',
   Watchman would melt.

At dinner parties he would try and steer the
   conversation onto things he didn't excel at,
   such as politics, heraldry or – ironically – Excel.

One day, he climbed Mount Everest –

But because he knew there would be a hullabaloo

He didn't tell anyone.

He just waited till the dead of night and then snuck
   out and climbed it (he wore lots of Gortex and
   crampons, and ate meat and candy to keep his
   strength up).

When he got to the top he planted his flag into the
   summit bit.

On it he'd written:

'It was nothing. I was mainly following all the other
   footmarks and in the last bit I used a can of air
   so I basically cheated.'

And then he sat down on his tea tray thingy and
   slid all the way back down, howling as he slid.

'SW19'

70   Roger Federer[23] won Wimbledon.

Sue Barker went to kiss him.

Federer –

Who felt invincible –

Turned the situation into a French kiss.

Sue Barker initially tried to resist.

Then she succumbed.

Her calves tensed and her heels pierced the turf.

◇◇

[23] I think you have to have a deal of respect for what Federer's done in the game. To win that amount of Grand Slam titles whilst your wife resembles an owl that much is quite impressive. Sampras's record in the majors was good, but he was playing relatively unburdened. Federer has now out-achieved Pistol Pete, and all the while with that sharp-nosed, saucer-eyed cretin perched in the stands. Great effort.

[24] I've only ever caught two fish and one was an eel. To this day I have no idea if that counts. If an eel is a fish suddenly, then where do you draw the line? Ducks, otters and water lilies might consider themselves no less a fish than the eel. Aside from this mangy eel, my only other catch was some kind of unidentified foot-long silver thing we landed in Sydney. It was a real wriggler and it took my friend Jonny about twenty minutes to kill it with his plimsoll. One of the other guys was recommending that Jonny pick it up and bash its head against the side of the boat, but he kept complaining that its neck was barbed and he didn't have the type of thick glove that would protect him. The blood was mixing with the water

POEM#479

'MEN AND FISH'

Roy caught an absolutely brilliant fish.[24]
He was elated.
He whacked it on the noggin with his carp mallet
    and cycled back to his fit wife.
She was overjoyed.
She threw it in the pot, whipped off her tracksuit
    and had Roy screw her in celebration.
They dined in ecstatic silence.

*

On the same day, Greg Range – a fish –
    Lost his son.
He organised the other perches into
    a search party.
Nothing.
He swam under a rock and lit a candle.
And then he wept and wept until his gills swelled up.

◇◇

in the boat and I took charge of keeping the girls calm. Not easy when
they had flecks of blood on their skirts and blouses. After some time a
silence descended on the deck. It became clear that the beast had been
slaughtered. One of the girls harvested its flesh and wrapped it in her
shawl. And later that week it was barbecued and devoured with Australian
lager and rice salad.

'FREDDIE'[25]

72 Freddie Flintoff scored 155 runs!
At one point he clonked a six, wandered up to
   Shane Warne and went, 'How did you like that,
   you womanising shit?'
Eventually he got out when Glenn McGrath
   bunged him a Yorker.
Freddie's stumps went everywhere.
He marched back to the pavilion, snuck into the
   Australian dressing room, did a gigantic shit in
   Glenn McGrath's blazer pocket and went for a
   curry with Steve Harmison.

◇◇◇

[25] The Ashes, 2005. I was at this match. If memory serves, it was at Edgbaston or the Oval, or it was an amalgamation of the two, or at the very least it was a distillation and reworking of everything that happened that glorious summer. Michael Vaughan doesn't appear in this poem, but that's not for want of trying. I really wanted Vaughany to be in this because I think he's the greatest living Englishman, but I couldn't think of a way. I spent about a fortnight trying to crowbar him in, out of respect as much as anything else. One day I hope to meet Michael Vaughan. If I do I'll go right up to him – I couldn't give a shit who he's talking to at the time – and I'll grab his hand and I'll say, 'Michael – you're the finest man in this whole bloody country, but you're a bugger to get into a poem, so you are.' It will be interesting to see how he responds.

POEM#1190
'YARDS'

Terry drank a yard of ale.

The pub went wild.

So Terry drank another one.

People were filming him on their iPhones.

He pounded his chest and drank another
    two yards.

He was a big fella and started smashing
    into things.

He carried on drinking yard after yard until
    closing time.

One of the locals worked out he'd drunk over
    400 yards –

Just under a quarter of a mile.

He could barely stand up.

The front of his Aran was damp with
    his slobber.

One of the barmaids was trying to confiscate
    his car keys.

POEM#746

'A BIBLICAL HERO'

74   David – the absolutely minute boy –
Stood in his baggy clothes (because there were
    none small enough to fit like normal clothes).
He'd been challenged to a fight by a man called
    Goliath, who was basically a giant.
He had a fierce face, too, and sawdust for brains,
    so wouldn't be reasoned with.
It would be like – nowadays – Frankie Dettori
    having to fight with someone who's medically
    a giant (Martin Johnson; the chap who played
    the Green Cross Code Man).
And also Goliath had a gun and a car exhaust
    pipe that he was swinging about.
David was petrified but didn't want to show it in
    front of all the people who were cheering at the
    Colosseum place where it was being held.
Goliath shot David about twenty times and hit
    him on the bonce and his brain wiggled about
    in his skull.
David didn't have a chance.
Then suddenly he crouched and collected
    a stone and slung it in Goliath's eye when
    Goliath was facing the other way.

Everyone went mad as David showboated,
    doing wanker signs at the stricken giant
    and strutting around doing impressions
    of Goliath and other contemporary giants.
That night David got off with the best girls
    in Jerusalem.
Goliath drowned his sorrows on mead.
His phone clogged up with horrible, goading
    texts from all the folk he'd annoyed over
    the years.

POEM#575

'AN ACCIDENTAL HERO'

76 June – the five year old – couldn't stop laughing.
She found her papa's appearance completely
   hilarious.
His beard, his specs – the hat!
He was a bloody nutter!
She pulled at her brown skirt, rocked her head
   back again
And laughed like a drain at him!

THE THORNY ISSUE OF JOBS

There's only one definite in life: everyone needs to get a job. Be you a surgeon, a masseuse or a gentleman who makes windsocks, you *will* need a job. I remember when our careers adviser came in when I was at school. He was a funny little man and he hauled a long, articulated trolley full of box-files with all the possible jobs in them. He stacked them all up around him in the corner of the library he'd been allocated and one by one all the fifth-formers went in there, sat on his knee and discussed what they might do in their working life. When it got to my turn I was bursting with excitement – eager to know what job I'd be doing for the next forty-odd years. We talked for a few minutes about my hobbies and interests and he asked me which subjects I enjoyed the most and what sort of grades I was getting. He was rubbing my palm with his thumb. When he felt he'd got all the information he needed out of me, he popped me down on a beanbag and started scouring his box-files for the perfect job. 'You sir!' – he finally declared – 'shall be a baker, sir!' I hadn't expected that at all. I couldn't cook and hated wheat with a passion. He'd specifically asked me whether I excelled at Home Economics and I'd been very clear that not only were my grades bad but that I'd had a problem with the teacher because I kept opening my oven too early and swearing when she handed out the aprons. I told him that I couldn't possibly be a baker – that it wouldn't be fair on the villagers who would be doomed to buy their bread off me. The careers adviser looked mortified and backed away and crouched in the corner. I asked him what on earth was wrong and he said that he'd had enough, that his job was a farce, that he 'hadn't got one right' for years. I told him that I didn't know what to say. All I could do was gape. 'Be a baker, you bastard,' he hissed. 'Say you'll be a baker.' I helped him back onto his chair and wiped the tears from his cheeks and promised that I would become a baker, and, petrified that if I didn't, he would find out and it would break him for good, I resolved to honour this pledge. I worked hard in Home Economics that term and got part-time work in a bakery that summer. Of course, it wasn't for me – I kept forgetting to put the gloves on, and burned my palms, and I would regularly lose my concentration and pipe cream into the head baker's hat. But I stuck it out for a couple of years and I don't regret it one bit. I'm glad I did it, for the weird man's sake. Of course, these days I make ends meet through poetry (supplemented by theft and voiceover work), but, to this day, whenever I see a cake, or bread or a till, I do allow myself a little smile.

POEM#96

'MISS D.H. FRENCH'

'I've come about the job.'

'You're fired!'

In between these two incidents,

Donna earned over £1,000.

POEM#941
'THE SHAKE-UP'

80   Bill Gower

Got a job as a doctor's receptionist.

He swapped all the magazines for porno ones.

People initially found it quite embarrassing.

Ultimately they adapted.

'THE WORK ETHIC'

Nancy – a prozzie – won the lottery
But carried on doing her job for the love of it.
Because she was now "fucking for free"
   she doubled her client list overnight.
All the other prozzies were furious.
Her pimp wasn't overly impressed either
   because he used to take a cut but now she was
   doing it for a hobby he got nothing at all.
In the end – because Nancy was one of those
   people who likes to keep everyone happy –
   she started charging again.

'AN APPLICATION'

82   I went into a shop
And demanded a job.[26]
'I'm going to sell all this stuff!'
The stand-in manager said something complex
    about application forms and having to wait till
    the main manager came back from her lunch.

◇◇

[26] I've had some good jobs over the years. I taught English as a foreign language to Swedes and Turks for a bit and I once worked as a workman. There were about ten of us and we had to dig a pit. Some of the lads brought in their own lunch. There was also a café nearby that served sandwiches with two sausages in them and I tended to go down that route. We got that pit real deep. In 2000 I applied for a job as a spy. In the interview I had to demonstrate how close I could get to a wall. They were interested to see what sort of job I could make of hiding against a flat surface if the man I was following suddenly got suspicious and spun around. I also had to lie without twitching and seduce the secretary. I assume they found someone sneakier in the end because I didn't get the job. Altogether, I have held down forty jobs, including positions as a P.A. to a shepherd and as a fruit picker, and I got paid for hiding stuff for a gang when I lived in Ukraine. That was fun work, but irregular.

POEM#943
'POOR DONNA'

Donna –
The receptionist –
Tried to eat some of her plum.
But she forgot she'd got her telephone headset
    thingy on
And the plum banged against it.
And the plum bruised.
And Donna cried her eyes out.
And Mr Grey sent her home.

'LIBERTIES'

84   Roy said,

'Help yourself to anything'

To the babysitter,[27] Nicki.

She helped herself to the reindeer meat that

    he'd planned to cook for his fellow cavers the

    following night.

Roy came home and lost his shit.

'I meant the biscuits and treats,' he implored.

She licked her chops and looked at her feet.

◇◇

[27] I've done some babysitting in the past. I used to babysit Terry. I'd get there and Marie (fit) would tell me that Terry had already gone to bed. She'd stink of perfume and make-up and she would often be wearing *actual fur*. Before she left – for some high-end dinner or piece of Ayckbourn – she'd show me all the Mint Clubs she'd got in and tell me to help myself to apples. She'd always come home lashed and reeking of champagne and men's aftershave. She'd palm me a tenner and kiss me, and off I'd go into the night, on my racer. This continued for about eighteen months. I'd babysit maybe once or twice a month. Always the same. Terry in bed. The stink. The fur. I never saw Terry. He never 'woke up' or 'came down'. After a year I began to get curious. I wanted to now what the little fella looked like, see what posters he had up, see if he wore fur. I crept up one night and pushed the door open, real quiet. Terry was shackled to his bunkbed, reading a James Herbert novel. He was in his late forties. 'Are you Terry?' I asked. 'Yes.' He seemed embarrassed. 'Don't tell her I was reading, mate.' 'No, of course.' I closed the door and went back down. When Marie came back she gave me the tenner as usual. I wanted to say something. I got on my racer but then got off and went back to the door. She poked her

POEM#269
'WANDSWORTH'

Wandsworth –
A bank clerk –
Got told about dress-down Friday too late.
He panicked, covered himself in foil . . .
   and was fired.[28]

◇◇◇

nose out. 'He was reading,' I said. 'Thank you,' she said. I rode off into the night.

[28] I got fired once. I was working at Hamleys – the toyshop – and got caught drinking half a Guinness at lunchtime. To be fair to him, the guy who got me sacked was a cunt.

POEM#688
'BUGWOMAN'

86   Bugwoman[29]

Flung tons of wet bits of web out of her wrists
and it all stuck to the scaffold.
A couple of bees flew into it and stuck to it
because it was gloopy.
Once they'd died, Bugwoman ate them.
Then she covered her wrists up with sweatbands
and went back to work.

◇◇

[29] I guess this one could have gone in the heroes section. I don't like this girl much, but it's pretty clear she's got a bit of the Spider-Man about her. Sure has his wrists, anyway. Maybe I could have put this one in the heroes bit and then shunted the Pinocchio one into the rascals section, or dropped it from the book altogether. Then again, I'm not sure this poem's a solution per se. Just because this bird's eating some bees it doesn't make her unequivocally heroic. It's actually pretty disgusting. Maybe the solution lies somewhere else entirely. Maybe I should have written a new poem. A poem about an Oskar Schindler-style figure who risks his job to help his fellow man on the sly. Yes, that would have been something.

POEM#869
'JON SNOW'

'When I point to things in the studio some
of them aren't *actually* there,'
Jon Snow boasted to the girl on the bus.
'So if there's a big pie chart coming out of the
floor, it's often the case that it's really just
graphics, not an actual, *physical* chart. But
of course, contractually I have to make out
they're there.'
The girl chewed her gum.
'It's difficult to explain,' Snow went on.
The girl farted.
'It's very weird for me, watching it back.'
Snow was floundering.

'DRENCHED'

88   Rob Decker's office flooded.

No one knew how – possibly a left-on tap;

> maybe someone fed a hose into the office and
>
> then turned on a tap in a different room but
>
> attached to the hose.

Either way, Rob Decker – who was, incidentally,

> tied to his swivel chair with posh Sellotape[30] –

Drowned.

◇◇

[30] I love this stuff. I don't think I've ever bought it myself but my flatmate seems to have an endless supply. I don't know whether he's peddling drugs in his spare time or *how* exactly he's getting the money together, but he always seems to have metres of this stuff. It's a bit like the Sellotape you or I would make do with except that it is slightly thicker and frosted. My flatmate also has lots of stamps. He has a lever arch file with pages of the bastards. If I ever need a stamp I don't need to go to the post office. I just wander through to Peter's room. He weighs my package and then starts tearing me the requisite value of stamps. The guy is compulsory! He also pays all our phone bills in full (rather than fannying about with a calculator and highlighter pens). And he cleans the toilets and taps. Oh, and did I mention he also has audio recordings of classic Olympic commentaries? You want to listen to Linford Christie scooping gold in Barcelona on cassette tape? Text Peter. Or, in my case, wander through into his room. He is quite, quite remarkable. Sometimes he polishes his shoes loudly when I'm trying to watch telly and one time he came home with an elephant's tusk that still had blood on it where it had been torn off.

POEM#806

'CHRIS HOCK'

Chris Hock (can you believe that surname?
   Hock? *Hock as a surname?*).
So this Chris Hock (!)
Won the lottery![31]
Four numbers.
Four hundred and fifty quid!
He immediately deep-kissed Liz.
He was so goddamn excited he also
   deep-kissed Nora.
After that it was pretty much open season.
He deep-kissed Karen, Rob Walsh and one
   of the cleaners.
People were diving behind their desks/locking
   themselves in meeting rooms et cetera.
Waiting till Chris Hock had calmed down
   a bit.

◇◇◇

[31] I don't play the lottery. I've got a friend who worked there and he said it was basically a swizz. The way he tells it, unless you're buying about 1000 tickets there's no guarantee of getting the jackpot. When I heard this I felt depressed as hell. He exaggerates, but even taking that into account you're still having to pump a hell of a lot of money in to be sure you win. Statistically, you're probably better off throwing your thousand pounds into the Thames and then hoping you're given a million pounds by a maniac a bit later that day.

'POOR FORM'

90   Alistair Darling went for a shit
      In the House of Commons swimming pool.
      All the other MPs got out.
      A lifeguard called security.

◇◇◇

[32] I think if I ever get my act together and get my own place I might look into getting myself a bee. I am well aware that some people think it is cruel to keep a bee if you live in the city, but I know that if I have one I'll make damn sure I take it out regularly as hell. I think my flatmate's starting to grow tired of me trying to convince him of the advantages of having a bee. He doesn't like to see me upset, but he's watched documentaries and had his head filled with prejudices so I don't think he's going to change his mind any time soon. What I need to do is take him round to someone who's got a bee. If I could get him into a situation where he's sat on a sofa, drinking merlot, with a bee on his lap, I think he'd soon soften. I'd wait

'A DILIGENT BEE'

Christopher Pound
Was the hardest working of all the bees.[32]

One year he produced eighty jars of honey.

Just to put that into perspective, the average was
    less than thirty jars.

And one bee only managed half a jar of the stuff.

In a whole year.

So eighty jars is loads.

When you imagine that each jar represents 250g –

That's loads of honey.

He also produced twenty jars of jam.

He was some bee.

As a reward he was presented with a cheque and
    some beautiful yellow boots,

And he got to have a go on the queen.

In his speech to the other workers Christopher
    modestly explained that his secret was never
    doing anything other than working,

And then buzzed 'My Way' to a rapturous hive.

◇◇◇

until he was stroking the bee's ankles and then casually drop it in: 'Isn't it something, Peter?' I think it would quickly become less a case of *whether* we get a bee and much more a case of *how many bees do we get?*

'BOSS/SECRETARY'

92   'Why do you never sexually harass me?'

'I don't believe in it.'

'Did you ever stop to think what I might like?'

POEM#1153
'THE OVERCLAIM'

Marge scrutinised my timesheet.

'You're claiming you worked 168 hours
      last week.'

I nodded.

'That's every single hour.'

I nodded some more and tried to smile.

'When did you sleep?'

I tried to think of something smartarse to say.

FRIENDS, ACQUAINTANCES AND WORSE

This is a section about those dreadful cunts – friends. Even the tiniest amount of research unveils that grim and unyielding statistic: *you can't choose your family but you can choose your friends.* Put it another way: *you are given a sister; you can scour your town to find an ideal friend.* Or: *your aunt may be a twat and there's nothing you can do about it; there's no excuse for hanging out with a dickhead who's not related to you by blood.* So if you've got your head screwed on you'll be picking up and dropping friends; constantly improving your slate throughout your life. I once made friends with a tall, Jewish man solely so I could use his van to help a girl move house. I buttered him up real good – took him to the cinema, cooked for him, let him have a go on my phone – and then casually popped the question. 'Say, Mike, could I use your van for a couple of days at the end of January?' He didn't have a clue. He came up with the usual hokum about 'what are friends for?' I just smirked and thought, 'Well, I know what *you're* for, Michael.' Once I'd moved Penny's stuff across town and had had my way with her in the back of the van, I returned it to Mike and shook his hand firmly. 'Whenever you need to borrow it, just ask,' Mike said. But my cogs were already whirring; thinking of who I could befriend next. I wandered across his lawn, hailed a cab and before you could say Jack Robinson I was drinking Guinness down the Eagle and scouring the boozer for my next conquest. *Every man jack* is nothing more nor less than a potential friend, and you're a fool if you're not cashing in. This section is all about these wretched individuals – the goons we drink with; those we turn to in times of need; those we pray we are sat next to at works' Christmas dos; those we steal from when they are at Kevin and Jane's wedding in America and we are house-sitting for them. Friends. Of all different levels of importance.

POEM#146
'THE LADS'

We clubbed together
And bought an annual.
It's about bird flight.
And now we hook up on Fridays,
Drink
And read it.

UNTITLED

98   'Westy, you swine!'
I confronted Westy.
'I can explain everything!'
And he could, too.
By the end of it I was shaking the bastard's hand.

POEM#406
'FUN'

Wanda Marshall

Drank 100 vodkas.

Other members of her drinking club applauded

and cuddled her.

She was so very sad.

'TOO MUCH ALL AT ONCE'

100   For some reason everyone texted[33] John.

There was no rhyme or reason to it.

Just everyone John had ever exchanged cellphone
    numbers with all thought of John at the same
    time, and all texted him.

So John got 440 texts:

'Hey man – you've got my Fargo DVD still'; 'Me
    and Jen just realised we haven't seen you for
    fucking ages – let's do something about that!';
    'John, do you have Ron Welch's number?'

John went through so many emotions that
    morning he lost twenty pounds in weight.

That's about nine kilos.

---

[33] I tend to send about half a dozen SMS texts per day, and I maybe draft two or three others. It's usually a fairly even split between texting people I know and entering competitions/using services designed to allow single people to flirt with one another. The company that I use charges £1.50 a pop, which, when you consider what the girls I'm flirting with look like, represents pretty good value.

POEM#577

'THE BANTER'

'I know what you've been saying about me.'

John Rib's face was red.

Lewis Stamp, Griff and the Page brothers sat
    on their camping chairs.

John Rib's breath was thick with gin.

'And you're wrong.'

Lewis Stamp smirked.

John Rib punched a bike and the clang
    reverberated around the garage.

'I do follow all of the banter.'

John Rib was shaking.

'If anything, I follow it best of all!'

POEM#613

'CUPID'[34]

102   Dave Pin-Willis ate a hundred and ten pies.
Gladys Tongue ate a litre and a half of posh ice
    cream and cried herself to sleep.
This was a week before their date.
Now they are soul mates, fuck buddies,
    and regularly host dinner parties.
So – well done me.

<><><><><><><><><><><><><><><><><><><><><><><><><><><><><><><><><><>

[34] Someone once tried to set me up with someone. It was really all just one big con. My contact was incredibly evasive when I tried to get photographs of the proposed date. All he would do was sketch voluptuous women, scan them and email them to me. This was no use to me. When I arrived at Pizza Express I showed the girl these sketches. She didn't know where to look. I was waving them in her face, shouting, 'You see how I've been stitched up?!' She reached for her rucksack and pulled out a similar wad of sketches – of handsome, muscle-bound men. She was ripping them into shreds and throwing them in the air, shouting, 'LIES'. I started doing the same. It was grim stuff. As we lay in bed that night, she described the scraps of falling paper as 'horrific confetti'. I thought that was cute. Very poetic.

POEM#617
'A SIMPLE OFFERING'

Chad bought me the latest shirt.
'It tells the time,' he whispered.
'I don't give a shit if it wipes me arse, mate,'
    I shot back.
'You're still not coming on holiday with us.'

'MATES' RATES'

104 'Scratch my back.'

'Twenty quid.'

I frowned like anything.

Twenty quid sounded so goddamn expensive.

That was what bugged me.

'Twenty quid' he said again.

I arched my back in the hope of catching my
   shoulder-blade against the coarse fibres of
   my pullover.

Anything to gain some relief without paying
   through the nose.

'Could you scratch it for any less than twenty
   quid, Malc?' I asked.

Malc smiled his toothy old grin.

I felt for my wallet in my handbag.

And I eyed Malc's long nails.

And I gritted my teeth because it all itched so
   goddamn much.

POEM#880

'PAT VS MATT'

Pat spat on Matt.[35]

Why did he do that?

Because Matt had bitten the snout off Pat's rat.

---

[35] Friends can fall out. I once punched my friend in the face a couple of times in the middle of Center Parcs. I felt like I was in the wrong, because he hadn't done anything to provoke me and because he was unconscious by the time of the second impact. When we had all returned from paradise I decided to buy this goon a bottle of champagne. In the event, the shop I went to didn't have champagne, so I ended up getting him four bottles of WKD, one of which I drank on the way to his house. The point being, it doesn't really matter how you treat your friends, it's about how you claw yourself back into their affections.

'THE GUYS'

106 'I am playing football,'[36]
Said Winston.
'And I am playing football,'
Said Chris Mild.
'I am playing football.'
This was Ethan.
'And I am playing football,'
Said Stuart.

◇◇

[36] I'm a great footballer. I used to play centre forward for my school team (we won the school's cup in 1993, defeating Linton 2–0 in the final at the Abbey Stadium) and had trials for QPR, Watford, Sheffield Wednesday and Werder Bremen. All of these teams decided that my audacious talents would upset the applecart. They recognised my genius but felt that I wouldn't fit into the systems they had in place. This was around the period that Kevin Keegan bought Faustino Asprilla to Newcastle and, though precociously talented, the Columbian had proved as disruptive as he was electrifying. I was a victim of my time. Since turning thirty, I have reinvented myself as a deep-lying midfielder. Similar in style and ability to Xabi Alonso, I tend to take the ball off the centre backs and then – nine times out of ten – I tend to unleash an inch-perfect pass to one of my strikers, who tend to then round the keeper and slot it home. Aside from football, I do no other sports. I find in other sports that the ball is too small or too hard or is conic and made of feathers. I hate having to hold a bat or a bow and I refuse point-blank to act out that ridiculous charade of putting on gloves before I hit someone. I tried skiing once. I found the whole thing lonely and painful.

'I am playing football,'
Echoed Brownie.
'And I am playing football,'
Said Geoff Cluster.
And now they'd all said it.
And Erick took the throw-in.
And they started playing football again.

'THE REUNION'

Herman grabbed Alfred by the lapels and
    spat, 'You don't change do you, Alfred!?'
Peter and Suzan – the ones with the white
    hair and fat, red lips – pulled them apart.
'Fuck yourself, Herman, or you'll feel my
    car keys in your face!'
There was a standoff.
Bill – who'd organised the reunion –
    sat eating his doughnuts in the corner.
Eric continued to get off with Tom in
    the kitchen.
Tom's black spectacles rested forlornly
    in Eric's upturned hat.
Robert and Bernard drank Magners out
    of plastic cups and moaned.
'This is a disaster,'
Bill whispered to Anita.
But she wasn't listening.
She was more interested in talking to her
    work colleague, Kerry, whom she hadn't
    really been allowed to bring along anyway.

'THE NOOK'

I found a new nook in my house.

I organised a hide-and-seek party.

I went to hide in the nook.

Rod Wilde was already hiding there.

'The whole point of this party was for me
    to hide there!'

Rod just didn't get it.[37]

◇◇

[37] Some words about my own friends: I have twenty friends. They are a mixture of (i) old friends from school, (ii) colleagues who I have been for a drink with a couple of times and it's got out of hand, (iii) my father, (iv) people who have shafted me in the past but who I persevere with and (v) a tiresome man called Ali (who lives in Buckinghamshire and has two young boys and one Irish wife). I'm pretty happy with this tally although I've got my eye on one or two others. I get on well with the bar supervisor at my local pub and I like the look of Prince William. I suppose the trick with Prince William would be to become friends with him before he becomes King. Otherwise you run the risk of him thinking you're only there because of his position. My plan would be to become pals either now or when his old man's on the throne, then when Charles snuffs it William will be shitting himself and saying things like, 'Oh, bloody hell, I'm going to be King now – this is horrendous', and I'll be playing dumb and saying things like, 'Fuck – of course you are – I'd forgotten you were royalty – I just like drinking bitter with you and hearing about your love life.'

POEM#578
'THREES'

110   Me, Brendan Worth and Laura Chen were
      playing threes by the park-bit by the pit.
'Can I join in?' Oh my God – it was B.J.
'No,' I said.
'It's threes,' Laura said.
'So piss yourself,' Brendan said.
B.J. spun his wheelchair round, used the slope
      to pick up speed and headed back to market.
Brendan[38] kicked a can and shook his head.
We started the game back up.

---

[38] I think Brendan is an arsehole, by the way.

POEM#394
'THE TRIP'

Elvin, Jonathan Chorus, T.T.L.R. Robertson,
   Ian and his new squeeze, the Willet sisters,
   Erica Vaughan, Tom's lot, Warren and his
   boyfriend (the optician, not that other
   arsehole), Chris, Khalid, Jessica and the old
   man from the cinema[39] went on a weekend
   away, during which Elvin unfortunately died.

<hr>

[39] The old man who worked at the cinema near me used to have a wig. All the kids called him Wiggy – but it was all meant in good jest. One time they nicked it and exchanged it for a 'wig' made by scalping one of the cows who lived on the common. He wore this abomination for about a month. It was about the time that *Honey, I Shrunk the Kids* and *Innerspace* were showing. In the '80s or early '90s, I think.

POEM#429
'COMMON INTERESTS'

112   Brian Hills and Ian Fisher
Both saw the same escort.
She had no idea they were squash partners
    and best friends.
She thought something was wrong with her
    head when they started using similar phrases
    during sex and recommending the same
    music over dinner.

POEMS SET ON LOCATION OUTSIDE OF THE UK

The UK's great but you'd have to be an idiot not to gradually become aware that other countries also exist. Belgium, Iran, Uruguay. Also Scandinavia and Japan. I could name thirty countries. I actually met a girl at a dinner party whose brother was married to a lady who was born in Mexico. I find all that sort of stuff fascinating. You also hear a lot about Australia and Australian people – and all this before I've even mentioned Zinedine Zidane. I suppose the lesson is: *be open minded*. I certainly try to be – I regularly buy phrasebooks and eat vegetables grown in Peru and, when new countries are discovered, I add them to my records and learn their anthems. When we were little, my brother had a globe that he could plug in and it illuminated. I used to sneak into his room whilst he was facing the other way, playing his trombone. I would tiptoe over to the globe and give it a good old spin, sending the countries into a blurred orbit. Then I'd prod my finger into it to stop it. Whichever country my finger landed on, I would then imagine myself on holiday in. Using this method I would spirit myself off to darkest Turkey and imagine myself strolling around the spice markets in my sunhat and shades. Or I'd picture myself playing the slot machines in Tunis or dream about being mugged in South Korea. Of course, now these dreams have become reality.

As an adult I am able to trot the globe almost at will. Last year I travelled to Hong Kong with a friend to attend a conference. Most of our time was spent in various seminars and lectures or trying to sort out getting accreditation or being sent to another part of the building to pick up lanyards. But one afternoon we did get to go and visit the tallest restaurant in the city and piss into urinals whilst admiring the vista. Our accommodation was riddled with mosquitoes and if you wanted to drink in the motel bar, you had to order food as well. I have also been to countries as far afield and exotic as Indonesia and (on a stopover) Bahrain. I still feel there's more to be seen, though. At time of writing I have never been to somewhere as rudimentary as Greece – which is an embarrassment for all concerned. For the sake of my art, I know I will put this right. For the sake of my art, I shall not be hanging up my money belt and travel Monopoly for some years to come. And as I trot, so I write.

POEM#517
'NORWAY'

Jack pulled his black trunks up over his belly
   and waded in.
He knew his car keys had fallen out of his pocket
   whilst paragliding over *this* fjord.
But he appreciated it could take days or even
   weeks to recover them.

'IF ONLY THEY HAD KNOWN'

116 Jaap Stam found himself sat next to Aled Jones
    on an aeroplane.
But neither of them knew who the other was.
So they didn't speak.
Not about press intrusion.
Not about nothing.
Jaap didn't even speak when Aled started crying
    because his ears hurt.

'AN ARCTIC SCENE'[40]

Oliver built his wife an igloo.
(They're both Eskimos)
Currently, he is smearing blubber on
   the ceiling.

---

[40] Great stuff. I love this guy. He's so bloody exotic – I think that's what I love about him. This handsome, leathery face deep in concentration as he 'smears' fat into all the little crevices to insulate his home. It doesn't say whether or not he has a radio. For me it barely matters.

'THE PILGRIMAGE'

118 Al slipped over in Bethlehem.[41]

He landed on a spike.

This ripped open his leg and rust went all under
his skin.

He wasn't so popular with the ladies after this
because – owing to incapacity resulting from
the injury – his weight ballooned and he was
grouchy at parties.

---

[41] I always prick my ears up when I hear anything about Bethlehem. I think it's because it's so closely associated with Jesus Christ. In case anyone's been living under a rock, Christ was born in Bethlehem (after a series of fuck-ups). In many ways he is to Bethlehem what Fred Dibnah is to Bolton or what Harry Redknapp is to London. I dread to think what kind of reception he would get if he came back down and booked out Bethlehem's equivalent of the O2 arena for his first public appearance. He'd bring the house down before he even spoke, I imagine. Of course, the world being what it is these days I imagine money might play a large part in where he did his first gig back. The States would be keen to have him, I'm sure, and oil-rich nations such as Qatar would see it as a chance of raising their profile and would, of course, be waggling pretty much a blank cheque under his nose. You would *love* to think that sentiment would get the better of him; that he'd forfeit the really big money and play Bethlehem . . . but I expect his agent might have other ideas!

'THE CRETAN BEACH'

'I'm just worried about you,'
I said to my daughter,[42]
Right in earshot of Ben –
Her treacherous
Husband-to-be.

◇◇◇

[42] I've never been lucky enough to have a daughter of my own but I've met a fair few over the years. My friend has a very polite daughter who she's raising in Sheffield, and my scout leader sometimes brought his daughter in. I once met a daughter who was nearly six foot tall, which, fair to say, I wasn't really expecting. You don't imagine them getting that big. I shouted out the words 'holy fuck' and then tried to cover it by coughing loudly and crouching. I was rolling about, pretending I hadn't been shocked by her height, but she had her head screwed on. Also, it was quite clear that I had said 'holy fuck' *before* I'd done the coughing, so she knew my game all too well. I was gasping and begging strangers for water. She was collecting her coat and making for the door.

POEM#33
'NOT ENOUGH'

120 'It'll take a sight more than that to win me back!'
   She screeched (we're from the States[43]).
   I stepped back into the Buick, fed it some gas and
      set off for the mall.

◇◇

[43] I have been to the USA.

'IN EGYPT'

Hassan

Juiced some papyrus and drank it on
    the veranda.
His Sphinx[44] looked up at him expectantly.
'No, no' – Hassan smiled, holding up a fist.
And the wretched creature sloped back into
    the pyramid.

◇◇

[44] My father was once bitten by a Sphinx in Egypt. He used to go away on business quite regularly. He went to Israel a couple of times and he also went to Rome. He always brought something back for us. Either from the airport or something more thought through. In 1990 he brought me back a keyring depicting the mascot of the Italia 90 World Cup – I still keep that on my keyring to this day. He would also do a slide show, showing us where he'd been. He had to shout his commentary owing to the loudness of the slide projector. Sometimes the slides would be upside down and we'd all contort our bodies to see it properly. This was funny. Ally McCoist sometimes did this on *A Question of Sport* when he had to identify an upside-down sportsman on the pictureboard. McCoist started only one game for Scotland in Italia 90, having been an integral part of the qualifying campaign.

'CHUCK JOSEPH'

122 A United States citizen

Got his hands on a gun.[45]

He drank his soda and made a list of some objects

   and people he'd like to have a go at shooting.

At first he was hopeless – missing a couple of

   trashcans from close range and getting his

   thumb caught in the trigger bit –

But then he practised on his brother a bit and on

   some cans a bit, and on the Sunday he went on

   a half-decent rampage – shooting the mayor,

   a couple of cows and a gigantic bell that rang

   and cracked at the same time when the bullet

   dinged into it.

---

[45] The last time I was in the USA I was visiting my friend Jason. We hired a car and drove to somewhere near Boston, Massachusetts. We went to a gun range. You had to sign forms and then you got given a gun and some ear protectors and moved through onto the range. I fired the gun at a target and because the gun was powerful my arms shook with each shot. If I'd been so inclined, I could have turned the gun on Jason or – worse – myself. It was an actual gun, so, with care, you could really blow someone's brains out.

POEM#412

'THE VALLEY OF THE KINGS'[46]

Bedecked in white shawls
A local tailor floated across the hot sand on
    his camel (Otto).
Nearby, a handsome Englishman
Fingered an Egyptian girl
Against a pyramid.

---

[46] That's two Egyptian poems. I have about eight Egyptian poems in all and flirted with the idea of having a whole section dedicated to Egypt (like the British Museum does). In the end I thought I'd be shooting myself in the foot. For every poetry-lover who is enthused by Egyptian considerations there are about six or seven who find it a turn off. So I just put two in and made space for some stuff about Israel and China.

'BORNEO?'

124   Jeremy Bailey's little plane crashed in the jungle.

He was stuffed right up the arse because he didn't
    have any water and he didn't get on with his
    co-pilot – who quickly stormed off in one
    of his huffs.

Jeremy Bailey put on his wellies and hats and set
    off looking for civilization, or a river to follow.

Anything.

For twenty days he survived on a combination
    of sticks, larger sticks, his own tears and
    a gentleman who had been ostracized by
    his tribe.

It was tough going but eventually he hauled his
    plane into a city and got enough reception on
    his phone to call a mechanic.

Jeremy Bailey sat on a curb and ate a pizza the
    size of a dustbin lid whilst this peculiar man
    in overalls smoked pot and fixed the plane up.

Jeremy Bailey paid this twerp.

Then he put his stupid leather helmet back on,
    hurled down his crusts and headed back up
    into the skies.

POEM#416
'BOYS ON TOUR'[47]

All the others went to Israel.
It was a package tour, where you got to see the
    birthplace of Jesus and Ronnie Rosenthal.
Wankers!
My mates – not Jesus and Ronnie.

◇◇

[47] This is based on my mindset in March 2003. We were all going to go skiing but it all went tits up. I basically read the emails in the wrong order, so I booked my tickets to Chamonix before I read the one where someone suggested we go to Israel instead, and the ones where the others agreed that Israel would be a good place to go. By then it was too late – I'd dropped three hundred quid on a flight to Grenoble and the subsequent bus. I tried to get them to switch back to the Alps but they weren't having it. I'm a stubborn old bugger, and I told the guys I wasn't going to switch to Israel, especially since I'd already bought the requisite equipment for a skiing holiday in Europe, online. They called me a fool and said I should come to Israel all the same. I said no thank you. I told them I didn't necessarily want to be plodding through Nazareth in salopettes. I wrote this poem in a stinking mood in a fondue café that backed onto a red slope.

'BANGKOK BELL-ENDS'

126 Owing to a mixture of youth, greed and stupidity,
Annie and Walker shoved a bunch of drugs up their
    arses and tried to waddle through customs.
Walker was going bright red with the guilt and
    Annie was pinching his flanks and whispering
    for Walker to go pale again so they wouldn't
    get caught.
The walkways seemed impossibly long and Walker's
    back was drenching itself with rivulets of sweat.
They were almost on the plane when one of the
    drug dogs noticed they were both crying a bit
    and pulling at the hems of each other's blouses and walking
    like they'd shat themselves.
Initially, the police[48] officers seemed very reasonable.
Of course, they were strict, but they didn't shout
    and Annie was allowed to stroke the drug dog and
    they were allowed to take the drugs out of their
    arses themselves.
But, latterly, the authorities started being more and
    more serious with them and, ultimately, the state
    sanctioned their death.

◇◇◇

[48] I hate the cops, Thai or otherwise. I was just brought up that way. One
time, when were in the Lake District, my dad got stopped for speeding

POEM#645

'THE ROUTINE BREAKS DOWN'

B.A. was bellyaching.

He didn't want to go on no plane.

Murdock distracted him by doing a divvy dance.

Meanwhile, Face hit B.A. on the head with
    a vase.

It cracked B.A.'s head clean open.

He lost tons of blood.

Hannibal tried to staunch the bleeding by tying
    his smart trousers around B.A.'s neck
    as a tourniquet.

Face kept on tutting and pouting.

Ultimately, B.A. bled to death, and they buried
    him at the base.

◇◇◇

(my dad's obviously a legend). We were in the middle of nowhere so my old man killed the cop. We all had to help bury him (on the side of Green Gable). That sort of thing stays with you.

'FLOATER'

128   A leg floated by.

Repulsed, Helen spewed into the lagoon.

I kept on steering towards the caves,

And cursing Lunn Poly under my breath.[49]

◇◇

[49] Being a poet, I find myself abroad a lot. It's impossible to write anything of any real worth without having first sat against a temple or gaped at a glacier. But these cultural pilgrimages are very different from flat-out holidays. I barely go on holiday at all these days. I think it has something to do with becoming overreliant on family holidays when I was little. Every year, without fail, my parents would slap down a proposal to me and my brother about our latest family adventure. Nine times out of ten me and my brother would simply wave the plans through, and soon enough we'd be sunning ourselves in Scotland or tearing down some French motorway in search of a campsite. One time, we had to put the trailer tent up in a raging storm. They all struggled with the poppers and my old man was swearing his head off and trying to get the metal feet down and banging pole-bolts with his mallet. I was too young so I was put in charge of holding the torch and picking my hooter. Once it was up my dad realised that the wrong side of it was right up against a fence so there was no way of getting inside and drying off. He was going potty. A couple of French guys were trying to calm him down but he was swinging his mallet in their faces and staying stuff about their country, implying, amongst other things, that they have more storms than we do. My mum went and slept with the French guys and me and my brother slept in the car. A couple of days later we caught up with my dad. He had bought a visor and was perusing a château. We went to France about six times all

'DRIVE THROUGH'

The most beautiful girl in the world
(A Chinese girl)
Works at a toll booth on a motorway
(In Sichuan province).
Several thousand modelling agents have been
    through and paid the toll in the last five years
(Whilst she's been working there).
But never through her booth
(More's the pity),
So she's never been spotted.
And as the years go by, her eyes become dull
    and her allure diminishes.
It is almost too late.
The skin on her hands is toughening;
Her hair is becoming coarse.

◇◇◇

told; Annecy, the Dordogne, Dijon – you name it. We also went to North
Devon and one time we went to Norway because my mum had saved lots
of tokens from cereal packets. Of course, all good things come to an end,
and these vacations dried up in the early part of the 21st century. And
after that – slim pickings. I sometimes go on websites or write to travel
agencies but seem incapable of the sustained administrative efforts
necessary to convert promising starts into actually sunning myself on a
rock in Minorca or climbing up some fiddly trail in Peru.

A POEM ABOUT A MAN FROM DEVON, STRUGGLING DESPERATELY TO JUGGLE HIS TWO MAIN PASSIONS; THAT IS, HIS ENTHUSIASM FOR HIS GIRLFRIEND, ANITRA (FORTY YEARS HIS JUNIOR AND STUDYING LAW SOMEWHERE IN TOWN BUT LIVING WITH HIM IN HIS LIGHTHOUSE), AND HIS LOVE OF THE SEA AIR – IN PARTICULAR, A COMPULSION FOR HUNTING DOWN, TORTURING, KILLING AND EATING SEABIRDS OF VARIOUS SPECIES

'BONKER'S GAME'

Bonker
Built a lasso out of fishing line,
Trained himself up,
And started catching seabirds with it.
Terns, gulls, puffins –
You name it.
Then he'd boil them up and eat them.
He kept this all a secret for many years.
He thought if he told someone it might get
    back to Anitra –
And he didn't much fancy losing her.

WHAT SOME PEOPLE DO

Different people do different things. My brother catches up with his phone calls when he goes for a run. My flatmate, Peter, recycles. My dad's mate, Speedo, always wears a swimming cap underneath his bobble hat. I think these people should be celebrated (except the people who are doing awful things like spitting in shops or trying to have sex with cars). There's nothing better than sitting at a dinner party, bored out of your skull, and suddenly finding out that the chump next to you does something that you have never before come across. You may have lost faith, and are pushing your food about the plate and yawning like a Yorkshireman, when your hitherto dull neighbour mentions that, for example, he wears disposable nappies on long flights. This changes everything. You are suddenly filled with an uncontrollable surge of pride in the human race. You are not merely learning that this individual dresses like a baby when he's in the sky. You are having it reaffirmed yet again that we are all different, that we are not cut from the same blueprint, that we are complex characters capable of carving out our own paths through life. And whilst most paths might not involve the humiliation of having your wife change you halfway across the Atlantic, one man's does. And it is this that makes him precious. There does not exist a man with nothing unique in his approach to life. Even in a tribe there will be one man making his blow-pipe back-handed; one elder who shoves his fingers in his ears when he farts. I'm sure that must be true. At the table, I was so pleased to learn about the bell-end's nappies that I broadcast it to the other revellers immediately, and he was mortified. But, as I explained in several follow-up emails and in a note attached to some wine, I was not being vindictive. Instead, I was flagging it up as a good thing. I was viva-ing la difference. I also clarified, in all of my follow-up emails, and in the note attached to the wine, that I still laughed when I thought about him.

POEM#940
'RADIOHEAD'

Gareth really liked radio.

He liked things like Chris Moyles and
   Woman's Hour and Classic FM.
He loved radio.
In the end he swallowed a radio.
But then he found it went all crackly.

UNTITLED

138   Gayle
Stitched all her clothes together
To make an absolutely
Enormous sweater.[50]

◇◇

[50] You sometimes see people who make their own clothes. They're maniacs. I suppose it started with them making cakes and then they moved onto clothes because 'making cakes' simply wasn't enough any more. I know, for myself, that so long as there are places like Debenhams and Moss Bros I will continue to 'buy clothes'. Currently I am wearing jeans and a t-shirt with my own face on it. My hair is damp from a recent bath.

POEM#785
'AG'

Gomez invented a new language that just went
    'ag ag ag ag ag ag ag ag ag ag'.
He was dead chuffed, was Gomez.
And after that he just spent the whole time
    going 'ag ag ag ag ag ag' –
Even when he answered the phone.
Problem was –
No other fucker spoke 'Ag'.
And – worse – half the time old Gomez himself
    didn't understand what the fuck he was
    talking about.
But by now he'd forgotten near enough all his
    native Chilean.
So he was floundering in a dreadful language
    no-man's land –
Or, as he put it, 'ag ag ag ag'.

POEM#1035

'MOATY'[51]

140 Alvin West

Built a moat around his car whenever he

parked it.

He had a pneumatic drill and crates of Evian

in his boot.

He would also lock the car in case anyone

had the balls to 'swim the moat'.

◇◇◇

[51] Unfortunate title – it brings to mind the boorish rampage embarked upon by Raoul Moat. A bigger bell-end you would do very, very well to find.

[52] I once got into a row about tongues with a man who worked in the money industry. We had somehow found ourselves at a pub together, owing to a mutual friend, and I was fuming. Now I was stuck in an awkward silence with this moneyman as our mutual friend fetched more continental lagers from the bar. There we stood, leaning against a large barrel. Me in my jeans and Puma sweatshirt, him in his suit, his tie loosened, stuffing his face with Brannigans. There was no way I was going to break the silence – I had plenty to think about. If he didn't like it, then fine – he could come up with something. Eventually he climbed in: 'Do you know which animal has the longest tongue?' My initial reaction was that I didn't give a shit, but I doubted that that was exactly what he had on his card. I played along. I recalled an image from somewhere of a lizard flicking its tongue out and snaring a crane fly. I thought it was as good an answer as any but suspected this prick probably had some horseshit up his sleeve. Eventually I just went for it. 'Some lizard,' I said, combining it with a yawn. He shook his head and sighed, as if I were the prick. 'Go on then, mate,' I said. 'I'm all ears.' He

'FOR EASE OF LICKING'

Rick-Paul Burnett

Got an operation in an unofficial hospital
    where they added in a couple of extra
    vertebrae segments in his spine so he could
    lick[52] his thighs more easily.
After that he was always leaning a little forward.
This made him look more inquisitive and nosy,
    and so he got the odd hiding.
But at least he could lick his thighs more easily
    than before.

---

puffed out his chest and said, 'Giraffe'. I was furious. Furious with myself, for a start. Now he'd said it I could easily picture a giraffe licking high branches and chimney pots. On top of that, I was still furious with him for asking the question in the first place. And most of all I was furious with the fact itself. I hated the idea of the giraffe holding the record for tongue *and* neck. And I hated the fact that I'd not been taught that as an infant. I remember being five, six, seven years old and pretty much always talking about giraffes. Why had no one bothered to tell me about its fantastic tongue? Why had we sung songs about its neck, but no parent, guardian, nurse or teacher had thought that it might be of some use in later life to mention the length of its tongue? 'Interesting, eh?' This fat banker was still in my face. 'Not really,' I said. 'I found it interesting,' he said. 'Did you now?' Our mutual friend was on his way back from the bar, elbowing other goons out of the way as he pushed his lagers into a triangle. I leaned in to the banker's ear. 'In fact – I hated that fact so much, I think you've put me off facts for a lifetime.' Jambo put our pints down on the barrel and wiped his hands on his jeans. 'What's the story?' he asked. I gave daggers to his fat beast of a mate. 'Ask him,' I said.

'GOING MEDIEVAL'

Richard Feast

Suddenly got into medieval things and castles.

He bought fuckloads of mead and replaced his
   front door with a portcullis and a drawbridge.

When his missus came home, he got his army to
   pour hot oil on her through special slats he'd
   made on the roof.

She was furious.

She shouted the following to him:

'What's with you?!'

But he didn't react.

He simply leaned back in his chainmail
   and ordered his guards to bung her in
   the dungeon.

'ORDER'

Ballard

Handed the waitress the menu.

'I'll take the Singapore noodles please, petal.'

The waitress frowned and curtseyed.

'That's not on our menu,' she emitted.

'I know.' Ballard gestured to his own menu.

'You should order from our menu.'

'No, no. I'll take the Singapore noodles –
    from my menu.'

'You should order from the menu in the
    restaurant you're in.'

The waitress was blushing and curtseying
    like mad.

'Cute,' said Ballard. 'But I'll take the Singapore
    noodles all the same.'

The waitress wrote it down.

Ballard fixed her with a stare whilst
    she curtseyed.

He pocketed his menu as she bustled away.

POEM#1142

'LONGTERMISM'

144   Barry went to the shops and bought everything he
        needed for the rest of his life.
      The carrier bags were so heavy.
      He got chatting with Mrs York on the way home
        and, after twenty minutes or so, the handles
        sliced his fingers off.

'AN ATHLETE'S WOES'

Steve Ovett got kidnapped and then got
    tortured (but only mentally) and then got
    sold to a private owner.
One day, after about five years, the private
    owner didn't lock the cabinet properly and
    Ovett ran away for 1,500 metres.[53]
The private owner had a converted jeep and
    went after him.
He burned Steve's retro trainers and locked
    him away *forever*.

◇◇◇

[53] I was never given the opportunity to run the 1,500 metres at my school. We ran just about every other distance but never the 1,500. I ran the 800 and the 400 and the 100. Some of the kids also ran the 20. It was frustrating for me because I watched the 1,500 metres on telly and I imagined that I would be best at that. I wasn't great at the other distances but I used to watch Coe and Cram and Ovett and Elliott and I used to go to bed sure that, given the chance, I, too, would be able to excel over that distance. My dad brought it up at parents' evening and was told that given my ability at 800 metres and the cross country it would be unlikely that I would be anything other than dogshit at the 1,500 metres. Part of me wanted to prove them wrong, to carve up 1,500 metres in my free time, video it and post it on YouTube, see how footage of me breaking 3 minutes 30 would sit with them. But for various reasons – couldn't be fucked/YouTube was still fifteen years away – I never did it. One day I will though, once I'm finished with poetry, with travelling, with living like a king – I'll slip on some spikes, I'll wander down to the athletics stadium and I'll scuttle round that track like a man possessed. And it will be glorious.

'OVER'

146   Anderson set about building a ladder in order
      to climb over the wall.
He climbed over and jumped down.
But then he wanted to climb back.
He set about gathering materials to build
      another ladder.

---

[54] I hate this side of things. Damn modelling. Every billboard you look at these days is smeared with photographs of the beautiful. I think it makes it very tough for the rest of us. It is very difficult to open a magazine these days, or scrutinise a Special K campaign, without being confronted with example after example of jaw-droppingly stunning models. Increasingly, society is being hoodwinked into believing that nothing is more important than being as gorgeous as fuck. I think it's a disgrace. I was watching an advert only yesterday where a hunk was shaving. Dark, toned and, presumably, well hung, this Adonis was the face of this specific razor that cut the hairs off your face without nicking the skin. I just think that sort of stuff is senseless. It's cunts like us who are buying these blades so it should be cunts like us who are selling them. What I would propose is a new system, rather like jury service. Everyone has to do a week's modelling and all the companies trying to sell

'THE PLAN'

Stephen Bryant
Decided to whisper 'I love you' into
  someone's lughole.
He found a modelling agency.[54]
A leggy redhead pranced out.
She had massive lips.
Steve bottled it.

◇◇

us their damn products have to use whichever doofus they're given. There
are no models. The people become the models. So if you're selling a bra you
don't find some pouting madam to do it – you are just given any old Tom,
Dick or Harry who dons the bra and poses as best she can for some photos.
You want to sell a Merc? Fine, but the star of your ad's a slightly older fat man,
who makes a bit of a fuss as he gets in. You're flogging a new perfume? No
worries – here's the ugly lady you'll be filming spraying it onto her plump
neck. I think this system would be initially unpalatable. The large companies
would be furious and would whinge when they had to have a stinker facing
up their campaigns. And it would take a bit of getting used to for us – having
sinful-looking creatures selling us stuff in the ad-breaks. But my God, it'd be
worth it in the long-run. Worth it to make it acceptable to look unexceptional
once more.

POEM#516
'LAZY'

148 Pearl slept.

She continued to sleep.

So far she had been asleep for seven or
   eight hours.

She continued to sleep.

And she continued to sleep.

After three days she woke up.

She checked her texts, had a packet of Hula
   Hoops, wiped the drool off her cheek, climbed
   back into her hammock, shoved her thumb
   into her mouth and slept again.

POEM#83
'DIGGER'

The alcoholic, Nick Webb,
Spends his weekends digging tunnels.[55]
Linking his three houses up.

<hr>

[55] When we were little we sometimes went to my great aunt's flat. She had a hatch in the flat that you could crawl through. If you kept on crawling, after a couple of hours the tunnel got narrower and then, if you kept on crawling some more, you would eventually come across a little brown lever on the side. You had to pull that and the floor gave way. And then you'd just drop. It was quite scary because the drop was big and when you landed you were in the sea. My mum didn't like us going anywhere near the hatch but we still did it. My brother did it more than I did, though.

POEM#567

'THE SONOFABITCH'

150   There was a chap in the café[56] highlighting his
        phone bill.
    What a sorry state of affairs.
    'I pay yay much and you pay yay much and Ik and
        Bik to pay yay much.'
    Something rose up inside me.
    'I'll pay the whole effing lot!' I said, slamming
        my tea down next to him and whipping out my
        money clip.
    'Now put your highlighter away and show me
        the total!'
    Splitting a phone bill indeed . . .
    If he's going to be a petty sonofabitch, I'll pay
        the shitting bill!

---

[56] I once went to a café with my friend Jonny (the chap who brutally murdered the fish in Australia). There weren't any free tables and the seats were all either benches – nailed to the wall – or chairs that seemed to be glued or screwed down. We'd been walking miles, so I didn't much care for Jonny's suggestion of pressing on to another café further towards York town centre. So we sat our arses down here, on seats in different parts of the café. Occasionally he would try and communicate something about it being nuts that we weren't sitting next to each other. He'd shout, 'Hey!' and do zany faces, as if to say, 'this is nuts!' But my seat was stuck down and facing away from him and after a while I found it tedious to turn round and look at him and find out what it was he wanted.

UNTITLED

Tony had his surgeon stitch a heart-shaped light
   to the palm of his hand,
For when he waved goodbye to Louise.[57]

◇◇

[57] I love this one. It's so sad. The guy loves Louise so much. Poor fucker.

IN THE DEAD
OF NIGHT

O f course, people of my parents' generation (born in the '40s) have very set views about the night. Once it is dark, they think, the idea is that you watch something starring John Nettles, make a drink involving hot water and granules and then creep upstairs, turning lights and other electrical appliances off along the way. There they will lie down next to each other, shut their eyes and remain, prone, for somewhere between ten and fifteen hours. There is another way. The younger, more enlightened generations understand that once the sun's no longer on the scene, there is no need to feel compelled to chug back our Valium and keep a low profile. *Au contraire*. Some of the best incidents can occur under the cloak of darkness. If you have the spirit of adventure, or if you have a car, there is plenty to be done whilst the docile sheep of the community are curled up in their pitiful cradles, dreaming incoherent dreams. One time, in my late teens, I arranged to meet up with a girl, Imogen, and we walked across farmers' fields until, hungry and shivering, we found a barn. Another time, unable to sleep, I turned my bedside lamp back on and read my book. It was by a remarkable writer called Colin Dann, a gentleman who wrote literature about the animals of Farthing Wood; a renegade team of nocturnal bastards who agreed not to instinctively eat each other, but instead to work as a team, to escape the wood and build a better life for themselves elsewhere. When you get your teeth into something like that it's easy to see insomnia not as a curse but as a gift from the Gods. Other times, I've been awake at two o'clock in the morning at social occasions such as parties or initiation ceremonies. The point is, though it may seem easy to dismiss the night as a major inconvenience, a scary mess of owls and street crime, you should at least experiment with embracing it. My advice would be to drink a couple of Red Bulls, haul on a Gore-Tex jacket and stride *into the night*. Learn to love it. Work with it. And that's not me giving the green light to criminal activity. If anything, that's me giving the green light to sitting, stone-cold sober on a bench next to a village pond, eating a filthy kebab and contemplating what to do next with your life. Also – as a heads up – don't read this section at night if you scare easy. One of the poems involves a severed head.

'IN NOTTINGHAM'

Marie did a shit in a cemetery.
One of the keepers saw her,
Burned her
And scattered her.

'THE THICK OF NIGHT'

156 'Your arm's jutting into my flank,'
I whispered to my lover.
'Oh, eff off, Chris,' she slurred,
Still half asleep.
I frowned.
My name is not Chris.

POEM#477

UNTITLED

Todd started a fire.

Diane threw herself in.

Todd was mortified.

That wasn't why he'd started it.

He'd wanted his teachers dead.

Not Diane.

She'd straightened him out.

POEM#1146
'NOTCH'

158   'I think you just want another notch on your
              bedpost, Laurie.'
          Fuck.
          She was onto him.
          He frowned
          And stretched
          And encouraged her to drink her port.[58]

---

[58] Port's really quite amazing. When I first got into drinking it was usually port. Me and the guys would go thirds on a bottle of port and walk it down to the park. Then we'd sit on the swings and see it away. Useful to know, port is actually a stronger brew than your average wine – a couple of bottles of that stuff and you know about it. When we got to about nineteen we took on a new friend who used to mix hers with water. She'd drink it like it was orange squash – about one part port to five parts water, and sit there gloomily sucking it through a straw. We didn't wind her up about this because the atmosphere never felt quite right but, looking back on it, I feel a great deal of sadness for Anna-Mae.

'HALLOWE'EN'

Richard decided to give his missus a fright
    on Hallowe'en night.
He chopped his head off and hid it in
    the freezer.
But by the time she opened the freezer he
    was so weak he could barely say 'Boo!'
And there was that much blood on the ready
    meals that her main emotion was one of fury.

POEM#636

UNTITLED

160   I counted[59] my wife's hands.

'One, two.' I said. 'Two hands.'

She rolled over and faced the other way.

I think she knew I was avoiding the subject.

◇◇

[59] My brother has children and I am a very disruptive force. He has been trying to teach his eldest, Edward, to count for a while now. Whenever I go round there I get the lad into bad habits. I'll sit there – deadpan – chanting numbers in the wrong order, repeating numbers, missing numbers out. All sorts. Every time my brother thinks he's getting anywhere I'll be round and start putting together sequences like '8, 10, 11' or '26, 27, 40, 28'. I've even introduced some of my own numbers. The poor fella thinks there's one called 'chafteen'. He thinks he's got chafteen fingers. My brother hates this. Having to spend his weekends denying the existence of chafteen. It's confusing for Edward, too. Hearing there's no such thing as chafteen is about as earth-shattering as you or I hearing there's no such thing as twenty. It's difficult for the lad to get his swede round it. Especially when his uncle's so damn insistent.

'DREAMING'

I had a dream last night.

In it I was involved in the television industry.[60]

I joined the action at a party populated
    by celebs.

Martin Clunes and Neil Morrissey were
    insisting on 'being lit'.

The others were more down to earth.

I sipped Corona, stayed out of Clunes's light
    and tried to relax.

---

[60] I am involved in the television industry. I'd recommend it to anyone. All you really need to do is find yourself an agent, screw a couple of producers and you're basically away. Once you've got your foot in the door, the fringe benefits are enormous. I have only been involved for a bit and I have already met Geoffrey Rush, been to a party where there was free drink and been on the same group email as one of the guys from *Little Britain*.

POEM#836
'JELLY'

162   'I like jelly.'

'I don't like jelly.'

'I like jelly.'

This continued for about three hours.[61]

---

[61] I *do* like jelly. I love it, in fact.

'CAPRICORN'

Capricorn
Killed Michael, Rod and the dogs.
And then she came for me.
I shouted, 'Capricorn!' approximately
    a dozen times.
And tried to keep the beanbag between myself
    and her.

POEM#1179
'FLOODS'

164   The beautiful blonde girl on the N15 bus
        on 29 January 2011
Sat in her mac and tights.
She checked her phone.
She drank a bottle of Oasis.
She cried.
The bus weaved its way through the city.
The further east it went,
The more she wept.[62]

◇◇

[62] My flatmate thinks she was on the wrong bus. I doubt that. You don't cry if you're on the wrong bus. You get off the thing. I think it was something else. I think her date had appalled her or she'd witnessed something damaging. She was so pretty. I think I've only ever seen one girl as pretty as this (apart from in films/ladies' tennis). It was that Chinese bird, working at the toll booth. She was just different class, to be fair to the lass. When I handed over my yuan, her smile lit up the whole highway.

POEM#926
'4.20 A.M.'

Wilson cracked a joke.
Nicola laughed.
Then she put the knife down.
Then they went back to bed.

'RADOX'[63]

166   A badger stopped working nights.
He foraged in the day and napped at
      around teatime.
At night he just relaxed,
Vegged out in the set,
Having baths,
Drinking.

◇◇◇

[63] I love Radox. In terms of liquids of that sort of consistency I have to say I almost prefer it to honey. I'll get through two or three bottles of the stuff a week (I mix it with water and have baths in it). I seem to spend half my life skipping down to the shops to buy bottles of Radox. I don't mind though – the feeling I have when I hand over the cash and they slide over the Radox is ideal. Though I have to say if there ever was a situation where they started delivering it like milk I'd be signing up pretty much straight away; I'd love to be able to open the door in my dressing gown and bring in that beautiful, fresh bubble bath. However, until that time comes, I'll just continue to line the bottom of my trolley with Radox bottles when I enter the supermarket, before loading my other groceries on top.

POEM#272
'ENOUGH'

'I might eat you one day,'
My lover giggled after one of our sessions.
'You mustn't come here again,'
I said archly, and stared out of the
    caravan[64] window.
She was unhinged.

---

[64] I suppose, if you think about it, when you see a caravan, a lot of times there are people inside it, doing it.

POEM#1160

'THE UNIVERSE'

168

Barry put ink on the eye bit of Mr Walker's
telescope.

Mr Walker turned round to tell Barry about the
planets he'd seen.

Barry laughed his tits off and Mr Walker swung
round to his mirror.

'I don't need my assistant horsing about, thank
you, Barry!'

Barry nodded and the two men smiled at
each other.

They took a break and drank Hock and listened
to a record.

But the ink reacted badly against Mr Walker's
skin, and four months later he had to have his
face amputated.

'NIGHT TIME'

Amy licked her lips.

Then she licked my lips.

Then I licked my lips.

Then we slept.

RASCALS

Rascals! They're so damn naughty! From the cheeky bugger who whips your chair away as you're about to take your seat at a dinner, to the saucy so-and-so who dunks your iPhone in your Ruddles, right up to and including the brazen miscreant who drowns a Red Setter. These impudent sods, with their t-shirts untucked and a flash of mischief in their eyes. They're awful! And yet. And yet. Try as you might – you just can't stay angry with them for long. Sneaks, rats and liars; scamps, tramps and flat-out hooligans. These are the guys that we love to hate. The guys whom we are drawn to *even as we try to escape them*. When I was younger I was fortunate enough to hang around with a rascal myself. His name was Chris Wilde and some of his stuff was *legendary*. He'd think nothing of filling some poor sap's socks up with toothpaste or sending off to a website for fake parking tickets and slapping them on motorists' windscreens. I once saw him light a firework and lob it over a toilet cubicle! The little lad's face when he came out! Another time Chris did a crap in an Easter egg, sealed it up all nice and gave it to the guy who used to come and help Mr Hooper out with football training. When he got a bit older, Chris became maybe even more of a craftsman. He used to dress in military gear and when he had his game face on there was no use trying to talk to him. He'd just go all serious and then do one of his pranks – real deadpan. A couple of years ago he stunned a goose, tied it to a paving slab and threw the whole damn lot through a window at the local library. The goose was going mental! Chris just lit another menthol and walked away. I find that I like to surround myself with characters like Chris, for my own sanity as much as anything else. I associate with squares as well, but they can really sap your strength, so I find it's nice to have someone like Chris to fall back on if you need a proper laugh. Of course, if it were ever to get out of hand; if that fine line between audacious stunts and flat-out antisocial behaviour were ever to be crossed, then I would walk away. But that's the thing that Chris has; that most rascals have, in fact – he knows when to stop. And that's why I love him.

POEM#466
'THE CONFERENCE'

A Swede farted.

The other delegates winced.

The Swede winced, too.

Even though it was the Swede.

'BIG BILL WALLER'

174   Big Bill Waller

Broke forty per cent of the records in the famous
   hardback *The Guinness Book of Records*.

He had, for example, broken the following
   records:

Most tattoos, Fastest guy, Most winter Olympic ice hockey
   gold medals, Tallest man and Most pies in an hour and
   a quarter.

Or at least this is what he told the barmaid.

She poured him his cider and frowned.

She thought forty per cent sounded rather high.

POEM#733
'BOASTING'

'I've killed nine people.'
I believed him because he was sweating.
And because no one would ever think of
    saying nine.[65]
And because I'd seen him kill a couple of'em
    with my own eyes.

◇◇

[65] I've never killed. I don't think I have any moral objection to it, just never really got my act together. I'm the same with Sky+. I miss all sorts of good stuff on telly by not having it, but I've never been able to apply myself; to sit down and make the requisite phone calls and get the man round. I suppose, in an ideal world, I should set aside a morning and get both things done. Have a man fix up a dish and wire up my telly, and then cave his head in with a champagne bottle. Disappointingly, I can't see it happening any time soon.

POEM#834
'BLOODY CUSTARD'

'Custard – you goddamn fool!'

I was shouting at Custard.

He'd somehow contrived to glue the cat to the
   grandfather clock we'd inherited from Andy
   Philips (when he died of old age in 2005).

'*Prise* her off!' I yelled.

'Fetch your toolkit and *prise* her off!'

But Custard wasn't listening.

He was examining Ruby's whiskers and chuckling
   to himself.

POEM#471
'PITT'

Brad Pitt killed Andre Agassi.

He poisoned his juice!

How dare he?!

How dare Pitt rub out Agassi?!

Anyway, Steffi Graf[66] was furious and played
   an exhibition tennis match against Michael
   Chang to raise money for a plaque in honour of
   her poisoned-to-death husband.

---

[66] I've shaken Steffi Graf's hand. I would have liked to have done more, to be honest, but tennis players are very specific people and I sensed that 'just the handshake' was probably best at this stage. I'll never understand those men who don't go to pieces when they think about Steffi Graf. I find her an incredibly beautiful lady. I know there are campaigns against her nose, and I'm not daft enough to think that everyone is in favour of Germans. But look at her legs. Look at her record in grand slams. Hell, look at her husband. Ideal.

POEM #1102
'TOM'

178 Pete Moore set himself up as a peeping Tom.
He bought a camera and a cardigan.
And he found digs near a ballet school.
And he started perving the following Monday.

POEM#710
'APPLES'

Apples

Stole his wife's hair straighteners to give to Bald
   Perry as a joke!
I think that's terrific.
I know he shouldn't have done that but . . . ha!
That's funny, that is![67]

◇◇◇

[67] My flatmate is bald. I tease him. I sometimes suggest that he 'combs his hair with a flannel'. I've also called him a bald cunt a couple of times, and I often compare him to Peter Ebdon or an egg.

POEM#893

'A BUSINESS SCHEME INVOLVING DUCKS'

180 'I've got a business scheme.'

This was Larry Woods.

'I plan to cut all the tongues out of all the ducks
    in the UK.'

'That's not a business scheme,'

I said.

'Stop 'em quacking!'

'That's not a business scheme,'

I said again.

<hr />

[68] Jim Broadbent is the most ideal of actors. He is the most loveable, engaging presence on screen. Recently I watched Mike Leigh's film *Another Year*. It's a brilliant film. Swathes of it are depressing – there's a poor lass who buys a car, which costs a bomb to run – but Broadbent's character is merry enough. I know that Mike Leigh has pointed him in that direction but even so, Broadbent's come up with a splendid little performance there. Of Leigh's other films I'd pick out *Abigail's Party*, *Secrets & Lies* and *Naked* as three of my

'THE CHEEKY GUARDIAN'

Susie Dent and Jim Broadbent[68] were
   marshalling *Dictionary Corner*.

He'd brought in a hipflask.

During the letters rounds Broadbent made lewd
   sentences by ringing words in the dictionary.

'Broad Bent Sausage Action.'

'Tug me.'

During the numbers round Broadbent created
   his rudest word yet.

Dent blushed, gulped and drove both her hands down his slacks.

The Whiteley/Lynam/O'Connor/Stelling figure
   had to cough to get Broadbent to snap out of
   it and do an industry-based anecdote going
   into the adverts.

◇◇

favourites for various reasons – but best of all has to be *Nuts in May*. It's one
of his earlier ones and is set in Southern England and if you haven't seen it,
get your thumb out of your arse and get that bought. It's a very touching, very
simple, very funny masterpiece. I also like *On the Waterfront, Alien* and, away
from movies, The Rolling Stones and anything by Roald Dahl or Raymond
Carver or Jamie Oliver, and I quite enjoyed school.

'LOVEBOY'

182 Loveboy
Kissed 33 women.
He kissed Elaine
He kissed Marianne
He kissed Lou
He kissed Nina
He kissed Regina
He kissed Denise
He kissed Roo
He kissed Tabitha
He kissed Connie
He kissed Anneka Rose-Marie
He kissed Gladys
He kissed Stephanie
He kissed a large girl
He kissed Pippa
He kissed Gloria
He kissed Muriel
He kissed Cynthia Webb
He kissed Alison and Rosie
He kissed Cruella
He kissed Trudy
He kissed his GP
He kissed Miriam

He kissed Mrs Roberts

He kissed Candy

He kissed Annie

He kissed Gladys (again)

He kissed Callie

He kissed Maud

He kissed Yvonne

He kissed Kiki

He kissed Paulette

And he kissed a Latvian girl

And then he drank
    heartily from the stream.

And then he fed his cats.

And then he played
    chess with his brother.

POEM#897

'DUNK'

184   Edward Mark Warner

Took Gloria to a very plush restaurant.

Just to put it into perspective, the tables actually
came with a hob, and you got to boil up a
broth on the hob[69] and cook fish in it until it
was done (and then you would eat it as usual).

When the broth had warmed up

Edward plunged Gloria's face into it and killed
her outright.

She was still face down and bubbling when
Edward asked for the bill.

Incredible.

◇◇

[69] I went to Mongolia (Inner) once. To get there we flew to Beijing and
then drove. The roads were full of potholes and you could drive for hours
on end without seeing a soul. Our driver was a weather-beaten Chinaman
who smoked local cigarettes and wore a smart tracksuit. Some of the most
frightening moments in my life happened in that car. When we got to our
destination – an extremely shit town – we went to a restaurant where there
were hobs on the tables (that's the only reason I brought it up). Of course, it
was initially exciting to boil our own mutton and pak choi. However, with
time, we got used to the procedure and so were left with an empty awareness
of the blandness of the food we were poaching, and a resentment of the fact
that we were having to do it ourselves.

'GARY'

Gary Glitter
Sat on the shitter.
He was smiling.
I don't know what he was thinking about.
The obvious possibilities are his music career,
    children or what to do next with his life.

'ON THE EXPENSES SCANDAL'[70]

186 There was a big do arranged for all the MPs to
    discuss how wretched they were, and to eat
    humble pie about the expenses fiasco.
The press were invited and everyone had to drink
    and mingle and apologise as much as possible.
Hoon sidestepped a hack and waddled over
    to Ed Balls.
'Is this wine free?' – he asked.
'Dunno.'
'Mm.'
Straw poked his beak in.
'Might not be. 'Cos we've been naughty.'
'I don't think it is free,' Widdicombe squawked,
    sipping from her hip flask.
'Bollocks.' Hoon winced.
He replaced his wine on a tray and they
    'moved through'.
The waiters served up braised venison and
    potatoes and fishes in sherry.
But, increasingly, the MPs declined, for fear
    of having to pay.
Some gritted their teeth or gnawed at their lips
    from hunger.

Widdicome unwrapped her sarnies.

The Milibands winked at her and ate their
little yoghurts they'd stowed in their little
briefcases.

After a couple of speeches admitting they were
all wankers, the MPs spilled out into
the road.

Some confused, abortive hailing of black
cabs ensued.

There was no guarantee these'd be freebies.

Hoon turned to Balls.

'Do you know anything about nightbuses?'

Balls tapped his bicycle helmet and pointed to
his trouser clips.

Hoon nodded.

And he huffed.

And he set off on foot to his nearest home.

◇◇◇

[70] This poem was written as a reaction to all the politicians snatching money from the public to buy things to make their lives more fun. Soon it will be out of date and you will need to Google 'Geoff Hoon expenses scandal' or bend the ear of a village elder to make any sense of this one. It is political.

POEM#1159

'MIKE'S PROJECT'

188   Mike White stole a bat[71] from his father's cave.

He drugged it and tamed it and stitched a camera

   to its beak.

Then he trained it up.

After a month the bat was flying about town,

   taking photos of girls' bosoms and backsides.

Mike White couldn't have been happier.

As the months went by Mike's bat became

   more skilled.

The photos became crisper, clearer

   compositions.

And it also started to develop the photos itself.

♦♦♦♦♦♦♦♦♦♦♦♦♦♦♦♦♦♦♦♦♦♦♦♦♦♦♦♦♦♦♦♦

[71] Bats are amazing. They're different from all other birds in that they have a thin layer of skin covering their feathers. They can still fly fine but, because of this skin, and also the fact that they can hang upside down, they are technically mammals. Bats can't sing like other birds but instead have borrowed from their cousins the dolphins, communicating as they do through a system of clicking and squawking. Because they are mammals they are prevented, biologically, from laying eggs – they instead lay other small bats. These then grow from chick to adult, their skin envelops their plumage and the cycle is complete. Humans don't eat bats because they would quickly lose friends.

POEM#1071

'TOAD'

Rat fucked Toad.

Toad never told anyone and nor did Rat.

Toad became very rebellious and kept crashing
   his car.

He was very unhappy.

Sometimes Rat[72] winked at him in
   the courtroom.

---

[72] I was once invited to play the role of Rat in a university production of *The Wind in the Willows*. To be honest I would rather have played Mole (naïve, squinting, loveable) or Badger (studious, dignified, solitary). In the end, after much soul-searching, I turned down the opportunity to don the cricket sweater and have a long, thin tail pinned to my arse, primarily because Rat is such a prissy, patronising goon.

IN THE THICK OF MARRIAGE

I have never been married. Each time I come close I lose my nerve or am thwarted by a second party. One such situation occurred last winter. I was on a train from Manchester to London and a young Italian-looking lady got on board. I approached her and began talking to her about myself. Things moved quickly as we passionately discussed the day's themes, and soon the young man she was with had waddled off to fetch help. By the time he returned, however, things had developed, and the idea of marrying this poor European couldn't have been further from my mind. I staggered back down to the restaurant carriage bleeding heavily, my scalp sore, clutching clumps of my own hair. I squatted and sipped my bitter – picking shards of my spirited Italian's Orangina bottle out of my head. There's no fouler taste than that of warm Worthingtons after a fracas. This is the closest I have come to finding myself in a marriage. I have, however, met several brave men and women who have taken the plunge, stuffed rings on their fingers and 'got mucked in' – so I have a more than fair idea of what marriage is all about. Marriage is, it seems to me, a complicated guy. For every walk along a sun-kissed coastline, there is a bitter dispute about a spatula that is covered in egg. For every protracted, wholesome sexual encounter in the downstairs toilet, there is a misunderstanding regarding who had said they would go down to the post office to pick up the spade that was delivered whilst both members of the married couple were out at work. For every loving, rambling discussion about what to call a baby, there is a dreadful moment where the wife walks in on the husband, sat, dressed as a soldier, watching YouTube clips of Stephen Hendry winning snooker titles in the 1990s. It is a cliché to say that clichés are usually true, but I think that the cliché about marriage being full of ups and downs probably is true. Over the past forty years I have been lucky enough to have front-row seats to one of this country's defining marriages – my parents'. They married in a village in the early 1970s, an unlikely union of a humungous, bearded beast and a naïve Welsh Barclays Bank employee with an impressive tennis game and a heart as large as a rugby ball. If I'd taken the trouble to video them for a couple of hours a day over the past four decades and then edited the resulting archive down to a ninety-minute piece, narrated by Ken Stott, I think it would have been a documentary that people would have been very interested in watching. Theirs is a tale of mutual support, teamwork, weekend trips to Bruges, fruit-picking, wine-making and, every so often, getting a new bathroom or kitchen. Many of their finest hours involve hosting barbecues or attending fancy dress parties – spectacularly, they attended one of Ray and Barbara's dos dressed as Princess Leia and Chewbacca. Everyone thought they looked terrific, but there was concern as to why my father was dressed as Leia, and general confusion, as it was 1972 so no one understood the *Star Wars* reference. But that's my parents for you. Innovative, imaginative, enduring. A formidable alliance. Perhaps their greatest triumph is that they created and successfully reared myself and my high-flying brother, Jon. He is now a father himself, and I am a poet. We're great guys. This reflects well on my parents' marriage and on marriage as a whole. As for me, of course, I hope that one day I have the courage to grab a girl by the wrist and drag her up the aisle. Get some priest to officiate. Everyone belting out hymns and weeping at my bride's beauty. Until then I will make do with *going to weddings*. I enjoy this. I bask in the positivity of it all. And I sip Guinness. And I consider my own position.

POEM#813
'JOINT ACCOUNT'

194 'Let's get a joint account.'
But she had absolutely no money.
I bit her lip and drew blood.
And immediately we were arguing about *that* and
   not about all this joint account bullshit.

'OFF THE CUFF'

The best man didn't prepare a speech as such.
He decided he'd just 'see what came to mind'.
In the event nothing really did.
He was largely silent.
Once or twice he'd look over at the bride and
    groom and say,
'There they are.'

'TOGETHER'

196   Sean and Christine had a bath together.

It was appalling.

He had just played football and so he was
    incredibly muddy.

And she was marvellously fat so only a tiny
    bit of Sean was underwater.

'TRIFLE'

Ian Mint groaned

As Jenny whipped him.

Earlier that day they'd finished off the trifle from

    the dinner party for breakfast.[73]

---

[73] My old man's dreadful for having desserts for breakfast. He'll merrily polish off some apple crumble and not give too much of a shit about it. When he orders a banoffee pie for pudding these days my mum just laughs. She knows he won't touch the damn thing until morning. And yet she continues with the charade. Crushing the biscuits. Condensing the milk. Filleting the bananas. And then plonking it in front of my father for a few minutes before she whips it away and they dance through into the kitchen and they wash up and they listen to *The Archers* and they discuss the other villagers.

'DOUBLE THE FUN'

198 Peter told a couple of white lies and bagged
    himself two wives.

He treated them like royalty and was deeply,
    deeply in love with them both.

He had four children with each, all of whom
    became doctors.

Once they'd all grown up and moved out, Peter
    took a deep breath and came clean.

He slid open the partition that divided his
    two lives and encouraged his loved ones to
    approach each other.

It was a massive shock for both of them.

It made it no less strange that they knew each
    other a bit from choir.

In fact, Maggie had met Brigitte's husband
    once – and, looking back on it, remembered
    thinking it strange that he was the same man
    whom she was married to.

Peter giggled guiltily and continued to prepare
    the two ladies their lager and limes.

POEM#1062
'SILVER'

Morris bought his wife[74] twenty kilos of silver.

He just dumped it on her sofa.

She bounced up and got off with him until 10 p.m.

◇◇◇

[74] This poem's also about wives and marriage: Poem#832. My wife got red-eye in a photo/Then I caught it off her/So now we're both on antibiotics. Clearly not worth a whole page on its own, but nice to squeeze it in, I think.

POEM#362
'ABDUCTION'

200   John stared at his wife, hard.

She stood on the doorstep, her faded red
    suitcase by her side.

She looked down at the floor.

'I'll ask you again,'

John said.

'Where have you been for the last sixteen years?'

Claire swallowed and blinked and focused on
    her gym shoes.

'Well, John hasn't changed,' she thought
    to herself.

POEM#841
'ROMANCE'

Mike shoved his dick into Caroline.[75]

She was delighted.

She kissed Mike.

It was the perfect end to a lovely evening.

◇◇◇

[75] The classic. I've done it myself (London, 2006) and it left a sour taste in the mouth, to be honest. We had wined and dined one another in an inexpensive restaurant that served their food directly onto trays, with no plates, and we staggered back up to my place. I'd been gearing up to it all day and had washed my sleeping bag, so I was devastated to find that I had locked myself out. After that, it was a particularly awkward experience, stumbling around looking for somewhere quiet. Eventually we settled for a covered bit outside the front of a gym. It wasn't by any means position A. The wind kept blowing rain under the shelter and her hair started to go slightly curly with the dampness.

POEM#1169
'THE CURSE'

202   The vicar pored over the statistics.
Every marriage he had ever done had ended
      in divorce, or worse.
He sipped his Boddingtons.

POEM#286
'THROUGH THE PARTITION'

'You shouldn't use such a big spoon!' I heard my
    wife giggle through the partition.
I retreated to the golfing[76] range and struck
    some drives.
Clearly Luther or someone was now *feeding my wife*
    in the afternoons.

◇◇

[76] My friend, Ali, heard about a game called 'urban golf'. In this game, you
hire golfing sticks, go into the city centre and start smacking balls as far
as you can down the streets. He invited me to play and we drove to Leeds.
We played eleven – fairly arbitrary – holes. We counted a hole 'done with'
if a ball went through a window of a building with nobody in it, or if a
police officer appeared in the distance and we had to abandon that part
of town, or if there was death or serious injury. Ali had played before (he
wore plus-fours and a pink cravat and beret) and he absolutely thrashed
me, but I have to say, in spite of this, I loved that night. Absolutely loved it.

POEM#206

'HANKY-PANKY'[77]

204   Mario did some hanky-panky with his wife.
Then he went for seconds
With Keith Power's wife.

◇◇

[77] In common with many of my poems, I drafted this poem several times. I wrote and rewrote this one maybe ten, twenty times before I was happy with it. More. For all my obvious faults, I am at least a perfectionist. This isn't even the final draft, I don't think. I think it might even be the first draft, which, again, makes me wonder why I bother. An interesting exercise would be to print all of the drafts back to back, just to see the sort of shit I have to go through. I think people would find that kind of illumination of the process fascinating.

POEM#332

'IN LEICESTER'

'I don't want to talk about it,'
My wife sobbed.
I was waggling the credit card bill[78] in her face now . . .
'I don't suppose you do,' I spluttered.
And I cycled back to my lover.
My busty, frugal lover.

---

[78] My own father often fixes my mother a look over his spectacles when he manages to get to a bill before she does. She stands in her national dress, her hands behind her back, and listens to him reading directly from the bill. He reads every word out, including the reference numbers. When he reads the words 'John Lewis' he says it very pointedly because he knows it's expensive in there. Once he's finished reading the bill he folds it away. He doesn't say another word. He doesn't chide or punish her. He just files the bill, takes off his spectacles, smiles and goes through to the kitchen.

POEM#1099

UNTITLED

206   James attempted to murder his wife.
They ate trout in silence that night.
The awkwardness was palpable.

POEM#1167

'COMMITMENT'

Clark kissed his wife on their first wedding
anniversary.
On their second anniversary he kissed her twice.
On their third anniversary he kissed her
four times.
And on their fourth he kissed her eight times.
On their fifth, sixth and seventh anniversaries
he kissed her sixteen, thirty-two and sixty-four
times, respectively.
By their tenth anniversary he was kissing her 512
times and they both developed rashes and were
late for their dinner reservation.
On their silver wedding anniversary,
they perished –
Exhausted and thirsty.
Only 800,005 kisses into the contracted
16,777,216.
Blinded by romance.
Killed by mathematics.

'THE PROCEDURE'[79]

208   Tony had his surgeon stitch a heart-shaped light
       to the palm of his hand,
    For when he waved goodbye to Louise.

◇◇◇

[79] I know I've said it before, but I can't get over this guy, Tony. Poor bugger. Just hopelessly in love with this girl. But from her point of view, she's got to do what she's got to do. I totally see that. It's no use her stopping there with Tony if she's not feeling it. And anyway, she's probably too young for Tony, if I'm 100 per cent honest.

POEMS ABOUT A STARSTRUCK DOCTOR, A FAT CHAP KIPPING ON A MATE'S SOFA, THE DISCREDITED AMERICAN GOLFER, TIGER WOODS, AN OFF-THE-HOOK WAKE, A MASSACRE AT A BATTLE-OF-THE-BANDS NIGHT IN LEICESTER, A BORED TRUANTER, A FOOTBALLER, A FARMER, A HANDSOME YOUNG MUSICIAN GETTING SHIT FROM HIS PIANO TEACHER, A ZOMBIE, A CZECH, A MAN-FACED GIRL, A GENTLEMAN HEAVILY INTO GOATS, A FANTASTICAL ORPHAN AND A TEENAGE LESBIAN, WHO, AFTER BAKING, USES THE PASTRY OFF-CUTS AS A PLAYFUL CENTREPIECE FOR SOME SLAP-AND-TICKLE WITH HER NEW GIRLFRIEND

I n any poetry anthology, collection or compilation the process of gathering the poems into cohesive themes is problematic.

POEM#983
UNTITLED

Gwendolin made twenty mince pies.
With the rest of the pastry she made a skirt
And had Chloe 'nibble it' off after dinner.

POEM#1136
'OPPORTUNITY'

212   The Queen got shot in the guts.
        She went to hospital and they fixed her up.
        The surgeon kissed her on the lips whilst she
            was under anaesthetic.

◇◇

[80] I wrote this one three years ago in Chester (which is walled). I wrote it in a posh café where they had enormous fruits made out of the material china everywhere. Not really my style, if I'm honest. I prefer to write in beat-up cafés and community centres. I'm in the community centre at this moment. It's in East London and is full of books you are allowed to read, plastic chairs and characters. Nearby, an elderly, military-style man is inspecting a mural and leaning on his umbrella, which he is imagining is a gun. Beyond him a pleasant lady in silver tracksuit bottoms is teaching a larger lady in blue trousers how to use a sewing machine. Behind the counter a young man wears a beanie and sways slightly to the music, which he is playing off his own iPod. His jumper is long and knitted and his black jeans are tight around his strong, powerful legs. There is a hymnboard up next to him displaying the specials. Top of the list is a sausage-and-tomato casserole, and a bent lady is sat opposite me stuffing some of this business into her mouth. When she chews she leaves her mouth open, and if I were a betting man I would say that someone has

POEM#430

'THE VERY, VERY BIG MAN'

I met a guy who was six foot four and seventeen
    and a half stone – so a bit bigger than Tony.
He was so physically imposing – and without
    any of Tony's good humour.
Anyhow, he's now staying with me for
    a few days.
I'm just hoping he gets his shit together and
    gets the hell outta there before Lauren
    finishes her course.[80]

◇◇

used celery in this casserole. There is a fine line here between members
of staff and members of the community. For example, a grey-haired
gentleman just came in wearing a rucksack that was made in the era
where it wasn't frowned upon to have a metal rucksack. He took it off and
got himself a cup of tea, but now he's shuffling about the place, collecting
people's plates and putting newspapers back in the carousel. Also, it is not
unheard of for the pretty Irish girl to stop serving scones, walk over to a
member of the community and play chess with them for twenty minutes.
One time there was a lock-in. Everyone read the books and played with
the children's toys and got shit-faced and rejoiced. There is a spirit about
this place. And, chiefly, in the community centre *everyone gets mucked
in*. Everyone does their bit. I sometimes wonder whether I should slide
through into the kitchen myself, and offer to scrape some shit off some
dishes. Just barge past the man in the beanie and demand to be thrown
a scourer. I might do that one day. See how they like that. By and large, I
think they'd be very positive about it.

POEM#1038

'TIGER'[81]

214 Tiger winked at the barmaid.

And he nodded cheekily down at the area of
    her work-trousers behind which her vagina
    would be.

She fixed him with an icy stare and poured
    him another bourbon.

Tiger frowned and went for his iPhone.

He scrolled through photos and found one
    of him wearing the green jacket.

He waved it at her and simultaneously tried
    to brush her bust with his knuckle.

She recoiled and he pulled up a Wikipedia
    page explaining the significance of the
    green jacket.

Still nothing.

He clutched her hand and said he had his
    own caddy.

She muttered something about having to
    cash up.

He latched onto this and said he'd show her
    cashing up.

He whipped out a bank statement and a
    condom and waggled them under her nose.

Her jaw dropped.

Then her pinny dropped, too.

Then he marched her to his golf buggy

And his caddy drove them to the allotment.

◇◇◇

[81] Dear old Tiger. I have an American friend who played college golf with him back in the '90s. He tells a brilliant anecdote about how Tiger sunk a long, right-to-left putt on the seventeenth green, ran up to the hole, took the ball out, threw it to his caddy, pulled down his trousers and pants and *fucked the hole* for about a quarter of an hour. I guess he always had that side to him.

POEM#736
UNTITLED

216   Griff
       Had a spliff
       And so did Sexy Mandy.
       Another bloke
       Had a load of coke
       And twenty pints of brandy.

POEM#180
'GIGGING'

I crouched
With my band.
Purvis – my drummer –
Was hurt real bad.[82]

◇◇

[82] Not very nice. I've never been fortunate enough to witness a shooting myself. There's no knowing where they are going to happen, unfortunately, and so by the time you hear about it and hop in a cab there's nothing to see. As soon as you arrive you're pushed by cops and have to stand behind bits of tape. It's depressing. Stern men in black uniforms saying, 'There's nothing to see.' You're telling me, mate! The more inquisitive you are, the shorter they are with you, and, by the time you're forced out of the picture, you're almost ready to say them, 'Okay – this is horseshit anyway.' I think that the only way you can ensure that you get to see a shooting is, increasingly, to be the guy doing the shooting or the guy being shot. But, of course, both of these roles bring their own pressures.

'DIRTY DERRECK'

218
Dirty Derreck
Spiked a birdbath.
All the birds got too drunk.
They told each other
'I love you'
And clattered into the town hall.
Also, Michael – the largest raven in town –
Fucked a robin.
Michael's fault?
Not really.
Dirty Derreck's fault for swapping all the water
for gin and Carling.

POEM#1012
'LOVE'[83]

A centre back went to York to have sex with
   a referee's daughter he'd met at a dinner.
She was still doing her A-levels.
He played for a high-profile London club
   (not Arsenal) and had England caps.
She wore one when they fucked.

◇◇◇

[83] No idea who this fella is. It's definitely not Sol Campbell because he played for Arsenal. I then thought it might be Ricardo Carvalho or Matthew Upson. It didn't seem quite Carvalho's style and Matthew Upson also played for Arsenal when he was much younger. In the end I thought, 'Who cares?' It doesn't really matter who it is. We should just read it, condemn it and flick through to a different one.

POEM#716
'THE FURY'

220   'This table's unstable!'
       I waved my ladle.

POEM#579

'PENIS EYES'

'Penis Eyes!'

I didn't need to hear this from Mrs Cooper.

'Just teach me the piano,[84] please,' I said.

I started doing chords again.

'They don't even jut out like penises,'

I muttered.

◇◇

[84] I took piano lessons for a while when I was a kid. My dad always regretted never having learned an instrument and so it fell to me to be 'the eleven-year-old sitting at a large piano with an old lady stood next to him'. With hindsight it doesn't seem like a bad idea. Certainly the thought of me being able to sit bolt upright on a stool, like Victoria Wood, bashing keys and belting out whatever was on my mind does kind of appeal now. But, unfortunately, at that age I was far more interested in focusing on things like sweets and football stickers and football in isolation from stickers. And so when it came to the big day I failed my Grade 1 examination. I think that's fairly rare, judging from the responses I've had when I've offered up that bit of information. My mum was in the waiting room and I pretended the reason that I'd not been able to press C was because I'd had an asthma attack. I bawled and wheezed and she took pity on me and bought cakes and Lilt and took me home. Discussions were held and a decision made. I was not built for music. And I was released back into the park with my shinpads.

POEM#536

'DELIBERATELY GORY POEM'

222
Roy was mowing the lawn.

Just ever so slowly mowing.

Up and down.

Up and down.

Up and down.

Down and up.

Also – he didn't have a head (chopped off)

And there were vipers and scraps of lung spewing
out of his throat.[85]

◇◇◇

[85] Apologies. Not very nice.

POEM#1139

'KAFKAESQUEISH?'

Franz Kafka[86]
Bought an orange.
But it tasted exactly like a banana.
In addition, it was shaped like a banana and was
   yellow like the other bananas.
He stared gloomily down at his orange,
Appalled that it was behaving like this.

◇◇

[86] I did a play that was a new adaptation of Franz Kafka's *The Trial*. Sometimes the other men and women in the cast would say things were 'Kafkaesque'. I was never sure what they meant. Sometimes they said that the cashpoint was Kafkaesque and another time they said that the lady who hired us the rehearsal space was Kafkaesque. In truth, I don't think I know what Kafkaesque means. It didn't stop me joining in though, saying how damn Kafkaesque things were. And it certainly hasn't stopped me writing a poem inspired by Kafkaesqueness.

POEM#1141
UNTITLED

224 The girl who looked like Kevin Spacey
Studied her tube map and licked her lips.

POEM#258

'WALKING WITH WILLIAM'[87]

'How much for the goat?'

How dare she ask this even?

I clutched William's collar and pouted.

'He's not for sale.'

William and I left.

---

[87] I'd like to see this one turned into a poster. I like the idea of students buying it and pinning it up in their dorms. That'd be something. I used to be a student, myself. All that cider, all those ciggies and girls! Happy days. I sometimes go back to student unions just to see what's going down. I'll sometimes have four or five pints in a plastic glass and play on the quiz machine. I have a friend called Bonsai who once won a *quarter of a million pounds* on one of those things. Bonsai couldn't believe his luck. He kept high-fiving me and pulling on my scarf. It took over two hours to pay out! It was still paying out when we left.

POEM#1063
'UP'

226 Pat blew a bubble.

Then he climbed into it.

And he floated out of the orphanage.

SOME
PROBLEMS

I f you are anything like me (which ideally you should be) you will, from time to time, as you go about your errands – as you buzz from flower to flower – as you dart around – completing tasks, fulfilling responsibilities, meeting your aunt, cooking your dinner, going to your bed – you will sometimes have *some problems*. Don't worry. It's natural. In fact, in recent years, I have become quite obsessed with this area. It seems that, unlike more specific things like opera and carrying a double bed (which you can avoid by not buying a ticket or not becoming a removals man, respectively), *some problems* are by their nature unavoidable and, in modern-day life, more and more common. You can quite happily be wandering along next to the canal, eating your Crunchie, scratching your balls, enjoying the vibe, when a group of old men race past on rollerblades, shoving you into the water. *A problem*. Equally, it's easy to imagine reading about medical illnesses in your local library when, without warning, a large dog arrives on the scene and bites your feet and calves. Again – *a problem*. It's also perfectly possible to imagine a scenario where you are baking some eggs for your landlord when, without warning, your fridge door opens and a midget steps out and starts barking the names of all the bosses you've ever had, right in your face. *A massive problem*. The point is, problems always have been and will remain an annoying fact of life and we all just have to accept them and do our best to overcome them where possible. No man can boast of having 'no problems at all' except possibly someone like Matthew Pinsent – although I imagine even Pinsent occasionally suffers a split carrier bag or has to deal with a crazed fan ramming stinging nettles into his puce face. The trick with problems is not to let them stress you out. Rather, you should just accept them as an appalling fact of life and get on with it. Because for every problem we encounter, there will be something like ten really positive things. For every time that you are caught short and fill your knickers with your own waste, there will be ten occasions where you make it to the bathroom in time and can enjoy taking a crap and reading an old edition of Viz. Of course, on a more pessimistic note, it would also be fair to say that one of the biggest killers in the UK is still *problems*, so we should still continue to avoid them (even if it means causing them for others).

POEM#1106
'WITH VEGETABLES'

Paul Loud

Sharpened a carrot and stabbed his lover
   in the eye.
Then he removed the evidence.
He ate the carrot.
Then he ate his lover.
Then he ate himself.

POEM#492
'PLUMMETING'

230   Chris jumped outta the plane.

But he'd forgotten to do checks!

His chute wasn't on his back.

He texted the pilot.

'Throw down my chute!'

But it was a different pilot that day.

When he got the text Des texted back

    immediately, explaining this.

POEM#1000
'BAD CALL'

Albert wrongly analysed a situation.
He did half a dozen Heimlich Manoeuvres
   on a busker.
He was incredibly apologetic.
And he offered to help the poor bugger
   reswallow his heart.

POEM#621
'PAINT'[88]

232   John Cun
Painted all his stuff white.
He invited his girlfriend
   (Claire Stewart) around.
She was appalled.
She left almost immediately and texted
   John Cun this text message:
I've got white paint on my Uggs! I don't get you.
   You're an arsehole.

◇◇

[88] I think so far in my life I've painted about twenty walls, four of them twice. My dad's the painter, to be honest. My mum says he should have shares in paint but he's looked into that and it doesn't make a great deal of sense. His favourite flavour is Almond White but he's not overly fussy. One Easter he painted an old filing cabinet he got from the tip. It took him ninety-five tins of paint because he used two coats and also filled all of the drawers to the brim. Whenever I need a room doing, he'll burn down to London with his paints and brushes and get the job done. He sometimes jokes that he's as much my decorator as he is my father. I can definitely see where he's coming from. There have been times when I have accidentally introduced him to my friends as 'my decorator'. In fairness, he seems to like this.

POEM#142

'HOSPITAL'

I went up the hospital.[89]

They took off the plaster.

My leg looked brittle; they tapped it.

It crumbled away.

◇◇◇

[89] I like it up the hospital. I smashed my arm to pieces a couple of years ago and used to have to go up there quite a lot so that the guys could all take X-rays of it and frown. One of the doctors was a girl called Chloe. I only knew she was called Chloe because one of the men who pushes the trolleys called her that once. I always had to refer to her as Dr Clark. She was in charge of giving me drugs to make the pain go away and of coming up with plans of action for getting it better. When I first started going up there she was very professional. She wouldn't let me see what she was writing and she shied away from physical contact. After a while she softened and we'd kiss on the cheeks when I arrived and cuddle before I left. My arm started to fix itself and she referred me to a physiotherapist. I hated this so I got my flatmate to rebreak my arm. I laid it out on a table and he brought a George Foreman grill down on it again and again, even doing it once more for luck after I'd said stop. When I went back up to the hospital I was placed with a different doctor, Dr Moore. I never even found out his first name.

POEM#1087

'OLD MEAT'

234 Robin got in a box.

Then a workman mistook this box for the box
   he was supposed to be carrying.

So he picked up this box and took it to
   the warehouse.

Once it was at the warehouse the girls hauled it
   onto the conveyer belt and it moved serenely
   towards the cruncher.

Robin was rudely awakened by the heavy claws
   piercing the cardboard and scything into his
   flanks like a lump of old meat.

POEM#527
'IDENTITY'

Nathan was fed up.

He'd woken up and his face was pixellated.

Now his wife was threatening to leave him.

He plodded morosely to the courthouse.

He was interested to see if the other jurors[90]

    were also pixellated.

---

[90] Since he's retired, my old man's spent a lot more time up at the courts. He goes up there and sits in the public gallery, watching men getting sent down for being bad eggs. He's seen all sorts of trials up there – trials for theft, fraud, kidnap. He loves it. The judges all know him now, because he's always there, eating his sandwiches and clapping. They've even started asking his advice a bit. Sometimes the judge pauses before passing sentence and looks at my old man. If he thinks he's done it, my old man will raise his sarnie in the air and nod. He even got invited to the judges' Christmas drinks last year.

POEM#1078

''TWAS THE SNAP AWOKE HER'

236   The bleak businessman snapped his shoehorn[91]

    whilst trying to get into his escort's shoes.

The coarse crack awoke the pretty sex worker.

She verbally abused her client.

And then she drove both ends of the shoehorn

    into his two ears, hammering them home with

    her gleaming stiletto.

◇◇

[91] I once went to a seminar where one of the men doing the talks broke his pointing stick by gesturing too violently towards a projection of a graph. He asked whether any of the delegates had a pointing stick or, failing that, if anyone had something that could be used as a pointing stick. People rummaged about for something that might fit the bill and eventually a lady volunteered her shoehorn. The man was suspicious until she actually waggled it in the air, advertising its length. It was about 40cm long. It was passed forward and the man had a couple of practice points with it to see whether he would be able to continue his lecture with this horn. There was no question. If anything the horn was more effective than his original stick. At the conclusion of the talk he asked the young lady if he could buy her shoehorn and she explained that it had sentimental value as well as being an aesthetically pleasing piece of carved wood. He barked a figure at her, desperate to secure this damn horn. 'A grand!' The young lady took the shoehorn from the man and fondled it. The man was barely breathing now. He just stared and hoped. The young lady bowed her head and returned the shoehorn to her handbag. She checked her timetable, touched her hair and moved onto her next talk. The man staggered backwards and crouched by his video projector.

POEM#476
'FLAMES'

Robin stared into the fire.
The flames were dancing.
Robin hit upon an idea.
He plunged his whole head, including his ears,
    into the fire.
Quickly, he realised his mistake.
He withdrew his burning head.
His son put a damp towel over him and called
    an ambulance and, over the next three or
    four weeks, people rallied around.

POEM#401
'KEN'S LOT'

238   'I will not give it to you,'
Horace said.
'In fact—'
And now Horace swallowed the key.
Ken threw up his arms and spat through
    the bars.[92]

◇◇◇

[92] I have rarely if ever been to prison. It doesn't appeal in the least. I know there are these films that try to glamorise it slightly. You see films where the prisoners are allowed posters or can throw themselves into improving the library et cetera but I'm sure it's not all sweetness and light inside those things. I'm sure that when you actually got there you'd have to wear special dungarees and have to eat what you were given by the prison cooks. People these days compare prisons with holiday camps. I shouldn't imagine they're that bad but I still wouldn't fancy risking giving up everything I've got out here (mates, bike, iPhone) to find out.

POEM#421

'OCCUPATIONAL HAZARD'

Denise South –

The witch –

Sat on the toilet in agony.

Her knuckles were white and she clutched
   her pointy hat.

'Aaagh!!' she spluttered through the dire
   splashing.[93]

What had she put in the potion to cause this?

◇◇

[93] Awful. I don't like this sort of thing. I hate to think of shitting witches. I'll tell you which one I like. The one about the gentleman smearing his blubber on the ceiling on page 117. Different world really. I don't think I'll ever tire of considering that image. I suppose the closest thing we have to that is grouting, but it's not really in the same league. I flipping love Eskimos. I hate it when there's reports of them being hunted or displaced. My attitude is, 'Leave him be. He's an Eskimo. Let him get on with it.'

POEM#522

'THE CHANGE'

240   Aaren Woogle

Went down the deed poll office.

'I don't want to be called Woogle any more!'
   he declared.

'Ha! Fair play – what are you changing to?'

Aaren Woogle hadn't thought it through that far.

He panicked.

'Winky Turban!' he blurted.

On his way home he bumped into his barber.

'Hey, Woogle!'

Winky Turban corrected him and then broke
   down in tears.

◇◇

[94] Just thinking again about that Eskimo guy. I'm actually starting to think that maybe I already put that in one of my earlier books. I had a book published with a fawn cover that mixed poetry with recipes and other bits and bobs. I really think I might have put this poem in that. If that's the case that's a massive oversight.'

'THE WIZARD'

Rob Lyle

Had a wizard come to him.

The wizard pulled some tricks to make sure Rob
definitely knew he was a wizard – not just some
cunt piss-arsing about.

Then the wizard said he could grant Rob
a wish, and gave examples of wishes Rob
should consider.

Rob thought of one of his own (to do with Daphne)
and the wizard said that was cool.

But then the wizard started moving the goalposts.

He started being pervy and touching Rob's forearm
and trying to kiss his stomach.

He kept on using phrases like 'What do you expect?'
and 'No such thing as a free lunch'.

Rob was torn, but decided –

With a heavy heart –

To make love to the wizard.

And the wizard was cold with him the next day.

But the wizard granted him his wish.

And now Daphne's letting Rob sleep with her again.

But Rob is cursed with these thoughts of being
made love to by a wizard.

And that's it.

'WHAT CAN HAPPEN'

242 Phil Nottinghamshire
Tried to tip the waitress.
But she was so meek that she refused his money.
Impressed by her humility, Phil Nottinghamshire
   reached for his wallet and announced that he
   would double her tip.
He waggled a tenner in her face triumphantly.
She quickly became distraught.
All she had done was bring him his ravioli, smile
   graciously when grating the parmesan and
   bend her legs into a curtsey when offering him
   the bill.
She begged him to put his money away.
Moved by her raw display of emotion, Phil
   Nottinghamshire rose from his chair, took her
   in his arms and whispered deep into her ear
   that he was willing to give her 'every last penny'
   he had.
Stunned to her very pit, the waitress crumpled
   to the floor and beat the ground with her
   youthful, Lithuanian fists.
Her white blouse was heavy with tears (about
   three kilograms).

She wasn't deserving of such an overwhelmingly
　generous gratuity, she kept wailing.
Amazed by her sweet-natured dramatics, Phil
　Nottinghamshire acted on impulse.
He grabbed a knife and stabbed himself in
　the chest.
He was losing blood as he struggled to focus on
　the waitress's name badge.
'Eliza,' he murmured, scrawling weakly on
　a napkin.
'I leave everything to you.'
Eliza was overcome, asobbing and ahollering as she
　beat Phil Nottinghamshire's back and chided
　him for his unstinting altruism.
She tried to prise the will from his fist.
But could not.
And –
Not seeing any other viable alternative –
She tore off her pinny,
Sliced open her throat,
And succumbed –
Her pride intact –
On her beautiful benefactor's benevolent body.

POEM#159

'LOYALTY'

244

Stripe –

My faithful old dog[95] –

Killed the burglar.

And I took the blame.

I loyally claimed *I'd* ripped him apart!

◇◇

[95] I have been to countries where it is culturally acceptable to eat dog. I have also eaten dog. However, I have not eaten dog in a country where it is culturally acceptable to eat dog.

[96] This is based on a personal experience endured by a friend of mine. Of course I've had the decency not to name him. I've taken the hit myself: made the poem about me, laid *myself* open to ridicule as per. I don't care; I felt I had to protect the guy. It would do his marriage no good at all if his wife marched into his study, slapped a devastated paw against this incriminating poem, and asked him what he's doing fucking hippos. I don't care how strong your marriage is, that kind of thing takes it toll. No matter how much you use the phrase 'that was ten-twelve years ago' there's a chance that she'll become irrational; start bringing up other bits and pieces that she sees as similar. In my friend's case I can say with certainty that this episode was a one-off, born out of some very specific circumstances. He was in Germany, at a conference, and he had been struck with a bat a couple of times earlier in the day. Long story short, he'd gone there with certain expectations of what the conference was going to be like and then when he got there it just wasn't like that. He thought there would be more opportunity to mingle with the speakers, basically. They hadn't really made any promise of this in the literature but anyhow, that was what he'd hoped would be happening. Increasingly he would try to pin the speakers down after they'd done their talks, bother

'MOST UNWELCOME'[96]

There was an imposter in my bed.

I tried to stay very still.

I touched the imposter.

Its skin was thick, leathery.

I wanted to flick a light on, find out more about the imposter.

I brushed my elbow against its jaw.

What?

A hippo?

But how?

◇◇

them with his own theories on education. On one occasion he'd followed a couple of them to a Japanese restaurant and tried to sit with them. He'd used the phrase 'at the Madrid conference this kind of thing was considered the norm rather than the exception'. On the second morning of the conference he had grabbed a speaker's lanyard and pulled them towards the cafeteria. An organiser had witnessed this and gave him two tasty clouts with a cricket bat. After that it had been a blur for my friend. He lost his appetite and about three pints of blood and cannot remember anything from just before lunchtime until the moment covered by the poem. The way he tells it, he left the bed as soon as he realised there was this unidentified beast at his side. He knocked on various other doors in the hotel and was eventually taken in by an Australian who allowed him to sleep draped over her chair. When he returned to his room the next day, the bed was made and there was a massive hole in the floor. Whenever my friend tells the story he becomes very emotional. I always try to egg him on, though, make him finish the anecdote. People like to hear about it. I think it makes him a much more sympathetic character once you hear about his time in Cologne.

THE KEITH POWER CONUNDRUM

'I was working on the proof of one of my
poems all morning, and took out a comma.
In the afternoon I put it back again.'
Oscar Wilde (1854–1900)

'**H**ow do you write your poems?' This is something I've often hoped to be asked. The process of poetical writing is deeply interesting to me. A poet doesn't just fetch up his pen, waddle down to the pub, line up something in the region of four to seven pints and then set about writing any old shit in the hope that some day his scrawl will be read by the masses. That can no more be the process for a poet than it can be for a Grand Prix driver or a judge. On average a poem will take something between twelve and eighteen months before it's ready for outsiders to enjoy. Of course inspiration can strike at any moment, so the poet must carry pen, paper and something to lean on at all times. But be in no doubt, inspiration cannot be tamed. In that respect it is like a lion, a rat and some dogs. In the following fourteen pages you will see the kind of shit I go through before a poem is ready to be uttered in front of enthusiasts, published in a book or binned. The poet's struggle from the first dismal draft to the final polished gem is an

unforgivingly long and beastly one.

POEM#206

DRAFT I[97]

Mario did some hanky-panky with his wife.   **249**
Then he went for seconds
With Keith Power's wife.

◇◇◇

[97] The first draft. The key at this stage is just to get anything down. Lid
off, press the nib hard against the scrap and scrawl something. Anything.
In this case it happened to be about this Mario creature. There's already
something about the shape I like. The fun and games of the opening line,
and then the horror. The rhythm is good and it looks quaint on the page.
I reward myself with some haddock and a snooze. And then I go again.

POEM#206
DRAFT II[98]

250   Mario screwed Keith Power's wife
Then cycled back to his own wife
And did it all again with her.

<hr>

[98] The aim here was to tighten up the opening line. It had felt quite loose. Quite airy-fairy. I also explored the possibility that Mario had a bike. I remember considering that he might have a green Dawes mountainbike. Possibly the bike would be old or have a basket, something like that. It would have a large silver bell and drop handlebars that Mario had fixed on himself, as well as the original handlebars. Pleased with this draft though I was, I was still acutely aware of how far I had to go.

POEM#206
DRAFT III[99]

Mario kissed his wife.
Then dropped round some rowing equipment
To Keith Power's wife.

◇◇

[99] I had been poring over Draft II for some time (just under five weeks). More and more, I was considering the whole thing a little crass. I hated the world that was being described. It felt too carefree. A grubby reality, where it was considered okay just to bonk any Tom, Dick and Harry and cycle around guilt-free, one hand on the handlebars, the other waving a can of Irn-Bru above your head. I was disgusted with myself. This draft was an attempt to return to something a little more wholesome. A more loving world where marriage vows still carry some weight and people return oars and loud hailers if they borrow them.

DRAFT IV[100]

252   Mario snogged his wife.

Then dropped round some rowing equipment

To Keith Power's wife.

---

[100] I felt I'd gone too far the other way. 'Kissed' seemed lame, so I dropped 'kissed' in favour of 'snogged'. Snogged is much better. We can imagine Mario yomping down the garden path, his missus waving him off, her lipstick smudged up onto her cheek due to the roughness of Mario's tenderness.

DRAFT V[101]

'I want a divorce,'

Mario confessed to his wife.

Her knees buckled.

She buried her face in her petticoats.

Ever the optimist, Mario quickly texted Keith's
    wife with an update.

---

[101] I took a cottage in Essex and regrouped. I began to hate drafts i-iv, and resolved to adjust the focus of the piece and tackle possibly the thorniest of all issues – divorce. If I didn't tackle it now then when would I? I also placed the action in the 18th century, see what that would do.

POEM#206
DRAFT VI[102]

254   Mario porked

___

[102] It was late when I wrote this one. It is also unfinished.

DRAFT VII[103]

Marie Power,

A class-A homewrecker,

Seduced Mario.

Over breakfast she joked about their spouses

   and did impressions of Keith finding out.

◇◇

[103] At this point I started thinking it might be interesting to view the mess from the point of view of the lady. Fair to say, I was starting to get a little tired of Mario Shaw, trundling around on his bike and banging anything with a pulse. I found him too single-minded. Too red-blooded. Too much is written about primitive men who can't keep their balls in their cords. It takes two to tango. So I decided to turn my attentions to Keith Power's shocking wife. Her. Sat there with her shell-suit unzipped to her stomach, her brassiere on display, her cheeks glowing in anticipation. I considered the moment had come to turn the poem on its head and examine her part in the saga.

POEM#206
DRAFT VIII[104]

'You're home early dear! What a lovely surprise!'

◇◇

[104] As a writer you sometimes have to be open to new possibilities. I was getting increasingly depressed by what was happening between Mario and the Powers. Increasingly, it was a slog to try and resolve their issues through poetry. I decided I might freshen things up and approached a gentleman who could cast a new light on proceedings. I gathered up my materials and met a man called W.E. Hughes, a cheeky illustrator. In this bawdy cartoon, we are presented with the pain of the situation whilst also being encouraged to have a giggle. The relationship between Mario and the Powers is presented in a light-hearted way. Mario comes across as likeable; a rogue. Mr Power as a sourpuss. I see this as both a strength and a weakness. It's nice to see what the guys look like – and I can sort of see why Mrs Power's commitment to her husband had wavered. The development I saw in the work at this stage was exciting but also demoralizing. I knew that if I stopped here; if I presented this as a final piece, I would be tacitly admitting that the bawdy cartoon was a more versatile form than poetry. I couldn't have that. To have stopped here would have meant that, henceforth, any artistic idea I formed would see me

DRAFT IX[105]

Keith Power pulled off his overalls and lit
   his pipe.
He'd just been in charge of buying a card,
   which came up to his waist, and getting it
   signed by everyone for Sally, who was leaving.
Then he got on his moped and drove it home.
On the way he picked up fish 'n' chips and
   a romantic comedy starring Rachel (from
   Friends) for his wife – on whom he doted.
He was disappointed but philosophical about
   the fact that Marie, it turned out, had eaten.
And he didn't like to ask her why there were two
   plates, a candle and an overpowering stink of
   Lynx in the air.
His wife acted shiftily throughout the film.
But 'that's just Marie' was his only thought.

◇◇

phone up my gentleman and explain the kind of saucy picture I'd like him to draw. It would be no kind of life. I thanked W.E. Hughes for his time, I told him I admired his craft and I returned to my quill and my brandy to make another assault on the Keith Power poem.

[105] I went long. I wrote this in March/April 2008. And it did have something. I felt I was at a fork in the road. Do I leave it here? Leave Keith Power sat watching a third-rate romantic comedy – his wife by his side, her cheeks still glowing from her afternoon's excursions; Mario awaiting his moment to tiptoe down the stairs and out into the yard. Was this it? Had I nailed it? Or was there more to be done?

258

X

Mario hooked his penis over his waistband and rang
the bell.
Mrs Power answered and ushered him into the garage.
She shouted something vague up to Keith about
'a delivery' and that she had to go and 'sign for it'.

XI

'Mario's moving in.'
Keith Power looked up from his cabbage pie.
'Eh? How does that work?'
'He'll come in with me – you'll be in the spare room.'
Keith pulled a face.
'Brilliant,' he breathed, almost inaudibly.

XII

Marie Power told Keith she was bored of his tracksuit
top.
Keith said he liked it.
He liked it because it had the Coventry City
crest on the breast.
Marie called it 'a relic'
And made Keith put it in the charity bag.
That Sunday, Keith walked past Mario Shaw's house.
Mario was wearing the tracksuit top.
Washing his car.

XIII

Keith Power wiggled his key in the lock some more.
Nothing.
She'd changed the damn locks.
He started looking around for Mario's bike.
He wanted to stamp on the damn wheels.
Buckle 'em!

XIV

Keith Power, Marie Power, Mario Shaw and
Cindy Shaw
Went to a Danish restaurant
To celebrate Cindy's birthday.
Mario touched Marie's ankle with his foot under the
table.
And he fed her bacon when Keith and Cindy were
outside smoking.

XV

Mario tried to convince Keith Power's wife to
take him and Linda Goldberg's husband at the same
time.
He sent another email checking she'd got his
first email.
He kept Linda Goldberg's husband abreast of
developments.

XVI

Twelve bottles of champagne were delivered to
the Powers'.
'There must be some kind of a mistake,' said Keith.
'Why must there be? Why must our having champagne
be a mistake? Why must our lives be grey?!'
Marie was wearing a nightdress that Keith had never
seen before.
He no longer understood the lady he had married.

XVII

Marie Power gave birth.
The doctor handed the little fella to Keith.
He convulsed in repulsion.
'Why's he got thick, black eyebrows?'
Marie was exhausted,
Lank with sweat,
Weeping with pain.
'Why's he got thick, black eyebrows, Marie?'
Mario peered in through the window.
His own thick, black eyebrows quivered with joy.

XVIII

'I may as well tell you, Keith—'
Keith thought, 'Here we go.'
'I'm having an affair with Mario Shaw – the gentleman
we met at Anne and Barry's pancake thing.'
Keith thought, 'Are you now?'
'I thought I was better just to say it.'
Keith thought, 'Did you now?'

XIX

There were muddy footprints going up the stairs.
Keith Power's face fell.
It was bad enough that Mario was round.
But why was he allowed to keep his shoes on in the
house?
Why didn't the 'boots off' rule apply to Mario?

XX

The holiday photos came back.
Keith and Marie in Tunis.
Mario Shaw was in the background of one –
Peering over a local newspaper.
Keith Power shut his eyes tight, squeezing out
a tear, which hung on his lash.

XXI

Mario Shaw offered to do Keith's kitchen.
'What do you know about kitchens?'
Keith Power asked.
'I'd do it for cheap and I'd put the hours in, Keith.'
'How cheap?'
'Forty quid a day.'
Keith almost spat out his Heineken.
'Wait till I tell Marie!!'
He grinned.
'She's gonna go mad for this!!'

XXII

Keith was shaking the wig in his wife's face now.
'This is Mario Shaw's toupee!'
Marie was shaking her head.
'No, Keith!'
Keith was stamping on the wig now.
Yelling.
'Then why was Mario bald at choir practice
   this morning!?'

XIII

Mario Shaw staggered into the bedroom carrying
   Keith Power's wife in a fireman's lift – her body
   covered in chocolate spread.
Keith Power was sat on the edge of his bed in his suit.
Mario dropped his freight.
'You're in Gothenburg!'
'No, Mario. I cancelled my trip.'

XXIV

Keith's shirt was smeared tight against his chest with
   the sweat.
His sleeves were rolled up.
He wiped the blood from his hands with a rag.
He looked across the garage.
Shaw's head hung against his chest.
The gaffa tape that held him to the swivel chair was
   loosening with the dampness of his blood.

XXV

'Why did you just call me "Mario"?'
Keith said again.
Marie's eyes were darting about the room.
'Why did you just call me Mario?'
'I didn't – I said "Marie",'
She finally said.
'So why did you say your own name during sex?'
Marie's eyes started darting round the room again.
Sweat glistened on her chin.

XXVI

Keith was staring at his wife's fingers.
She turned another page of her chick lit.
He wondered where her wedding ring was.
She saw him gawping and put her book down
   and rolled into the kitchen.
Keith looked glumly down at the novel.
The Baker's Wife and the Randy Naval Officer.
He nibbled his ham.
His wife came back in and started reading again.
Her ring was back on.
That, at least, was something.

XXVII

Keith Power hacked into his wife's email account.
He emailed Mario Shaw.
'Whatever it is we're doing, I want it to stop.
   It's not fair on Keith.'
He signed out,
Wandered into the kitchen
And ate a whole Vienetta.

XXVIII

Keith Power drove west along Midsummer Avenue.
He listened to Carmen and ran through his
   presentation in his head.
Mario Shaw cycled east along Midsummer Avenue.
He had a wide grin splashed across his face and
   an erection.
He waved as he passed Keith's white Merc.
Keith pretended not to notice him.

XXIX

Keith Power walked in on his wife as she wallowed in
   her bath, hippo-style.
He noticed that her breasts were heavily tattooed with
   foreign writing.
He wondered what it meant.
And he wondered when she'd had it done.

XXX

Keith Power asked his wife why the Marmite had
   run out.
She said she didn't know.
Keith spoke in a low voice:
'You don't eat Marmite and I have stopped eating
   it as an experiment – to see if it still went down.'
Marie thought on her feet.
'It's me. I've started spooning a bit away each day.
   I don't know why.'
Keith stared at his wife.
She transferred her weight from one foot to the other.

XXXI

Marie Power asked Keith to wear a mask during sex.
'What's the mask of?'
'Oh, don't be an arsehole, Keith. Just tell me whether
   or not you'll fuck me in a mask.'
'Yes, then.'
Keith wandered unhappily down to the shed.
Increasingly, he thought, it was Marie calling the shots
   in this marriage.

XXXII

Marie Power went missing.
Her husband, Keith, couldn't find her anywhere.
He tried to get a news conference going in which
  he could describe her and plead for her to
  come back.
He asked *Crimewatch* to do a reconstruction.
He gave them casting suggestions;
Sally Hawkins as Marie.
Steve McFadden as Mario.

XXXIII

Keith Power bought candles and scallops and a banner
  for his wife's birthday.
He spent two hours cooking the scallops –
  in a beautiful potato sauce.
Whilst he cooked he kept receiving texts from his wife
  pushing her estimated time of arrival back further
  and further.
When she did arrive she was all the things Keith
  had dreaded.
Sloshed, full – and with Mario.
Keith had had enough.
He charged forward and knocked out Mario with
  a loud hailer.
He tied Marie to a chair and force-fed her scallops.
Occasionally he noticed himself humming
  'Happy Birthday'.

XXXIV

'Powerpoint! My man!'
It was that treacherous beast, Mario Shaw.
Keith Power felt his gun in his waistband.
'Hello, Mario,' he said, smiling grimly at what
  was about to kick off.

XXXV

Keith Power walked aimlessly through town.
His rowing tracksuit was damp with sweat and the
  breeze was chilling his bones.
He peered through the window of Pizza Express.
Couples linked hands across Margheritas
  and Diavolos.
He started to bang his forehead against the glass.
Lightly.
Rhythmically.

XXXVI

Mario came round.
He gave Keith Power a violin.
'Why are you giving me a violin?'
'Just because.'
Mario was torn apart by the guilt.
Keith Power shook his hand and clutched his elbows
  and hugged him.
'Thank you, Mario. You're a good man.'
Mario threw up in his mouth and swallowed it back.
He felt worse than ever.

XXXVII

Keith Power, Marie Power and Mario Shaw relaxed
  in bed.
Mario was smoking.
Keith and Marie were leafing through the
  broadsheets.
Occasionally Keith would read something out loud
  in a funny voice and they would laugh.

◇◇

[106] A frenzy. I took myself to Southport, bought thirty tins of frankfurters and fifteen loaves of bread and hired a caravan with a stove and a kitchen table. I then sat in my knickers – my pen in my fist – and scribbled like a madman. I knew that somewhere, buried, was the truth. A poem that would expose Mario for what he was – a grubby little chancer. A poem that would sing. Every two hours I would stop for sausages. Every three hours I would go for walks around the caravan site. It doesn't take a genius to work out that four times a day I was walking around a caravan site eating frankfurters off a paper plate. These pieces are the fruits of this long weekend.

POEM#206
DRAFT XXXVIII[107]

Geoffrey Rider sped down the motorway.

He couldn't work the tape player.

His cowboy hat kept slipping down and his
   gun was jabbing into his balls.

◇◇◇

[107] This represented a slight change of direction. Tired of Keith Power and his hideous wife and her hideous behaviour and Mario in general, I tried something a little different, involving a chap dressing up and nicking an Audi. It felt liberating to chronicle this man's life. It wasn't the solution per se. But it was cathartic and drew a line under Southport.

DRAFT XXXIX[108]

262   Keith Power sped down the Marie Power.

He couldn't work the Mario Shaw.

His cowboy hat kept slipping down and his gun
was jabbing into his rowing equipment.

◇◇

[108] This is the kind of mess you can get into if you're a poet. In an effort to return to the dismal narrative of the Powers' domestic problems, and in trying to preserve this new dynamic of the speeding cowboy, I ended up fudging both issues and found myself faced with a poem that neither condemned the Powers, nor celebrated the German automobile industry. This was an ugly poem, a horse-by-committee. I took it to a few readings at poetry cafés around London but the reception it received was fairly grim. I endured a month of this misery before I decided I needed to identify exactly where the jewels lay. After some thought, I decided to move back to the themes that had driven me to pick up my tools in the first place. I returned to Mario Shaw, and the destruction he wrought on the Powers.

DRAFT XL[109]

Keith Power dangled the tie in his wife's face.   **263**
'Whose effing tie?' he kept yelling.
He was bloody furious.
He was so close to calling her a snake.
'And why won't you let me check in
   the wardrobe?'

---

[109] The fortieth and final draft. Completed on New Year's Eve, 2009. It's stripped right back to its essentials. The sly, scheming madam leaning against the wardrobe. The portly businessman shouting through his tears. The pain of a marriage crippled by infidelity and the age difference. I love this poem. I love imagining that slap-headed sneak, Mario, encased in the wardrobe, quaking amongst the jackets.

ON THE OUTSIDE LOOKING IN

S ome people live their lives in the thick of it all. Things come easy to them. They waltz into the inner circle and never look back. They stand there with their 'good job' or their 'wife', and people 'listen to them' when they speak. We've all seen these guys. They probably have a car, a gym membership, a mobile chock-full of people who will return their calls and text back. But there are people for whom it is not quite that simple. For every individual who has the requisite clout to organise a Hallowe'en party consisting of more than twenty ghouls, there will be some poor sap sat on the toilet, on hold, trying to get through to a corporation to complain about being treated like a worthless ass. For every broad-shouldered gentleman, effortlessly getting a barmaid's attention and being served a pint of stout, there exists a man, thin and exhausted, plodding the streets, looking for love. I, too, consider myself an outsider. A Frankenstein's monster, cut loose and scared, condemned to drift from nightbus to café, from forest to stripjoint, in the hope that one day I will be embraced, warmed, fed and loved. Recently I earned some money through dishonest means and I have tried to reinvest it into penetrating the inner-circle. I bought jeans, cowboy boots, a frock coat and an iPod and have started approaching groups of young people, offering myself up as a potential member of their friendship group. I augment my case by buttering up these goons with crates of beer and inviting them to stay at my place whenever they want. I give them envelopes with directions to my flat, instructions on how to use my oven and keys, which I've had cut. By day I stroll into large open-plan offices, find a spare bit of desk and set myself up with my laptop. From these foundations I try and become part of the embroidery of whichever new-media company I have landed in. In my breaks I stand with the smokers, offering up my own fags and slagging off the boss. Anything to feel involved. Anything to get away from the outskirts. But I know, deep down, that it is on the perimeters that I belong. Leaning against the advertising hoardings, watching the game develop. Wishing I could don a team jersey and be a part of it myself. This section is for those poor fawns who find themselves in my boat – or, at least, clinging, with me, to the side of the boat. It is the final section of the book. And it is a hymn to the outsiders.

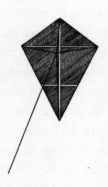

'STATS'

I'm in love with a girl.
But I'll never have her.
Or at least it's *statistically unlikely.*
Because she is extremely pretty.
And because I only saw her on the telly in the
   crowd at the French Open.

POEM#894
'PREPARATION'

268   Philip Brookes
Practised standing in front of his mirror.[110]
Once he was satisfied with the shape of it all;
Once he was confident that all the angles were
    pretty good,
That he didn't look like a complete sham,
He went to the station and stood in real life –
Waiting for Connie.

❖❖❖

[110] I used to have a teacher who claimed never to have looked in a mirror. We all found this staggering and had about a million questions for him. 'How do you know what you look like?' and 'Why not?' and 'Come on, Mr Wade – stop being a prick.' Some guys also took off their shoes and were throwing their shoes at him. In the end Mick Mason and Louise Steer locked him in his own store cupboard until he promised he'd stop saying he'd never looked in a mirror. Another of my teachers, Mr Lloyd, used to do up old Morris Minors. Two of the teachers at my school were married to one another. But they never held hands or made out in front of us.

POEM#962

'JIMMY'

Jimmy

Drank a half of Beck's Vier[III]

On the hour, every hour, for six months.

After only three months he was so pissed he was
    slurring his words

And texting Lucy.

◇◇◇

[III] Beck's Vier is only 4% in terms of its alcohol content. It means you can drink a little more. The key is not to go mad. It matters not if you're drinking Beck's Vier, Fünf or Sechs. If you're drinking dreissig of the buggers you're being a fool to yourself.

'THE END'

270 Mick Finch got to the curry[112] last.

Not his fault – he'd gone to get money and dump
   the kit at his car.

Now he was sat at the end.

He was sat next to Wardy's Serbian friend and had
   no one opposite him.

He spent an hour switching between staring straight
   ahead, chewing his saag

And straining across Branco,

Trying to join in with the banter about the waiters.

At one point he suggested that they mix it up a bit –
   give him a go at Eggsy's end.

But everyone called him gay and fired shards of
   poppadoms at him.

And though he hadn't even been allowed to move –

He now felt further removed from the action
   than ever.

◇◇◇◇◇◇◇◇◇◇◇◇◇◇◇◇◇◇◇◇◇◇◇◇◇◇◇◇◇◇◇◇◇◇◇◇◇◇

[112] In my line of work you spend the majority of your nights in curry houses. One time me and my mate got a bit fruity and asked the chef to go hotter than he'd ever been before. 'I'm not comfortable going that hot,' he said. My mate fronted up to him. 'What's the hottest you've ever been? 'Cos you can double that for a start-off.' When he brought it through a couple of the other guests left, overpowered. Me and Breeno just got

'SHARING'

A man with inwards hands

Found a man with outwards hands

On a website.

They met up.

They talked about their experiences.

They pumped money into a quiz machine.

They hugged.

They felt better.

◇◇

mucked in. At one point, Breeno had his whole face in the serving dish, snouting about for chillies and rubbing his stomach. In the end the chef drove us home. He bloody loved it. He kept on saying, 'Fair play to you boys' all the way back to the flat. When we rolled in, Breeno woke up my flatmate by jumping on his bed. He breathed into Peter's face, charring his eyelashes.

POEM #505
'ENVY'

Jeff Adder

Looked across at the couple by the window.

There was a chap.

He had a plate of lobster and Windermere
    carrots that looked absolutely bloody divine
    and he was rocking his head back and laughing
    heartily with a curvaceous redhead whose smile
    sparkled like sun-kissed cherries.

Jeff frowned and looked sadly down at his
    own meal.

And then sadly up at his own date.[113]

---

[113] Glancing across can be horrible. I saw a man on the Tube the other day and the green-eyed monster rose up in me. He was eating the most fantastic looking orange. I damn near lost the plot. I haven't eaten an orange now for nearly ten years, for one reason or another, and this bastard was colossal. He knew I was watching, too, and made a real thing about how juicy it was. He'd bite into it and then have his hand cupped underneath it as if, were his hand not there, his Blackburn Rovers shirt would be ruined by the sheer quantity of juice. I pretended not to be looking. I pretended I was happy with my boiled egg. Just sat there licking my egg and licking my lips and smiling.

'THE SPARROW'

A sparrow became obsessed with
  Emma Bunton.
He flew 1,100 miles to be with her.
He sat on her birdbath and she took him as
  just another sparrow.
But privately he was having some pretty dirty
  old thoughts.

◇◇

[114] Yup, it's definitely true. The one about the smearing Eskimo was in a book I published in 2007. Huge apologies. I hate the idea of it being in both books. I had just forgotten that we'd put it in that other one (*25 Poems, 3 Recipes and 32 Other Suggestions*) – that's a bad oversight, actually. Great poem though. I guess that's how it wormed its way through the net. The tenacious Eskimo, stretching up and insulating his home.

'A PROACTIVE MAN'

274   Griff Spence needed a wife.
       He'd done the wine bars thing.
       Absolute bullshit.
       He got to going door-to-door.
       In his third year he found a girl, Esther,
            who invited him in for talks.

POEM#726
'PURSUIT'

Aiden bought the girl with the kite

Twenty gifts.[115]

He arranged a time to meet her.

And he handed over the stuff.

She was unmoved.

She just chewed her gum

And had her husband bag it up.

[115] I haven't received a gift in over six years. People just don't see me as that kind of person. Sometimes it's even worse. People expect gifts from me. I hate that because I don't get any joy from giving. Recently I got an email from a friend who said she didn't like to mention it but she thought it was weird that she hadn't received anything from me for six months. I emailed back – said I only give presents when I have to – birthdays, christenings, muggings et cetera. She called me 'unacceptable'. I think that's scandalous – sending out emails, casting around for gifts. Truly dreadful. I went onto Amazon still seething and ordered a couple of books by Jonathan Safran Foer and a Joss Stone CD for her.

'STANDING BY THE SANDWICHES'

276   Lester arrived late at the orgy because of traffic.

Everyone already seemed to know each other.

He couldn't seem to find anyone to fuck.

He rubbed his hands against his hips –

Where his pockets would have been if he had

      been wearing trousers.

◇◇

[116] On average I'll draft a text message something in the region of three or four times before I send it. First, I'll come up with a concept, say, an idea. Something the text might be about. Usually regarding something in the news/something in my life. Then I'll sit down and compose something rough, save it into drafts and then go away and clear my head. When I come back to it, I'll have a look at what I've done and see how I like it. I'll maybe throw in another couple of ideas, jiggle it about a bit, maybe add something more current in – for example, if I'm eating some cucumber I'll mention that. Then I'll put it to bed for a while, go for a swim. When

POEM#891
'ANYONE?'

Ruby Danzak
Texted[116]: 'Who's up for it?'
To everyone in his phone.
No one replied.
Ruby vomited.
A couple of days later he texted: 'Did none
    of you get my last text?'
Everyone replied almost instantly.
'Yes' and 'Sure' and 'Yeah, I got that'.
Ruby texted again: 'So – come on then –
    who's up for it?!'
No one replied.
Ruby vomited.
He was at a loss.
He vomited again.

◇◇

I come back to it I might do final tweaks, or something a little more
fundamental, or even throw it out, start it again, if I think it's not up to
much, but this is rare. Then I'll send it to someone I trust – my brother, my
solicitor – and get a steer from them. They give great feedback so there's
usually some bits and pieces that will change at this point, but frankly not
much. By now I just want to get the message out there. From here, it's
fairly simple. I choose someone from my contacts list who I think might
find it relevant, import their contact details into the 'To:' field, and hit
Send. And then I wait. See if it hits the spot.

POEM#171
'LEAFING'

278   'I'm not marrying that pig!'
I said to Mother.
She continued to leaf through the portfolio.

◇◇

[117] This has been my curse. I don't pick up on signals or, if I do, I think the signals might have been sent in error, or I've misread the signals, or the signals are there but she's doing them more as a piss-take, like in the film *Carrie*. I once had a girl prise open my mouth and lick my tongue but because I found the notion of her falling for me too good to be true I assumed that she was possibly teasing, or that maybe she had Gulf War Syndrome. More recently, I have started to address the problem by using phrases such as 'Are you flirting with me?' and 'If I grab your thigh will

'COURAGE'

Chris-Chris

Sat with Dolly for almost over an hour.

It was all talking.

He wanted to kiss her but couldn't raise

    the courage.[117]

The irony being –

Dolly wanted nothing more than to kiss Chris-

    Chris or – at least – she'd've gone along with it.

But Chris-Chris didn't have the bottle, poor sod.

And he certainly didn't know that Dolly would have

    been cool with it.

And so it was that they merely finished off their

    soda and parted with a hug.

Chris-Chris kicked cans dejectedly all the

    way home.

He consoled himself with the thought that he'd

    have another crack at Dolly – maybe when they

    were both pissed.

But in the event he got caught up in some crime the

    next day and was shot dead – right in the chest!

---

you slap my face?' I can come across as blunt and socially limited but I'd rather offend and be glassed than to later be consumed by regret at not having tried it on.

'NOT SO WELCOME'

280   They advertised for a new flat mate and got one
   called Nikki.
But when she arrived, Nikki was in her seventies.
They remonstrated with her in the kitchen.
She kept saying she was young at heart.
She kept pouring herself muesli.
They tried to make her go back on Gumtree –
   share with some old-timers.
She said she was too old to be messed about.
She told them to stop swearing.
She wanted someone to take her coat.

'AT WORK'

She sat in the café.

Her hair was nice.

Like silk.

Her skin was lovely, and bloody smooth.

Her bosom was extensive without being
ridiculous.

Feeling a poet's gaze on her lips she shuffled
round and faced pretty much directly away
from him.

Her brownish-black hair toppled down her back.

You had to actually crouch down a bit and sort of
angle yourself around a bit to even see her legs.

She shot me a look and I threw down my pen and
pretended to be whistling.

I became aware that my coffee had gone cold.

OUTRODUCTION

You don't always get an outroduction these days but I tend to think they're quite important. I look at it as a form of aftercare and also basic politeness. I'm the same if I ever cook for someone – afterwards I sit them down and explain myself and apologise and cuddle them. And I'm the same if I kiss someone at a wedding or reverse into someone's car. I'm quick to swap details; I try to explain myself. I want them to be happy.

That's all the poems then. Thanks for getting through them. I know how bloody tough it can be to wade through poetry. It can be a nightmare, in fact. All that I would say is, if you think it was hard work reading, try writing the damn thing! However much time you wasted ploughing through this bastard – double that, and you're getting somewhere close to how long I spent getting the thing done. For me, this feeling is heavenly. To finally be allowed to leave my stool, take off my poetry clothes and waddle forth, back into society, is bliss. To be in a situation where I can at last bin my coffee cups, smack my hands together and fuck off down the pub – it feels sensational. It is at this stage that I will have my intern check for typographical errors and tighten up some of the imagery in the longer poems, and then she will send it off to my publishers for spell-checking and printing. And then, some months down the line, I will be reunited once more with the man in his thirties, and he will pass me the bundle and I will shake his hands. And this time

I think it will be my turn. My turn to buy him a breakfast. Or, if he prefers, my turn to buy him a hamper of cheeses and wines and nuts, or to enroll him on a kayaking course. And then I will retire to my corner. And I will unwrap the bundle. With great care and scissors. And I will do what you have just done. I will read it. And I will see what all the fuss is about.

INDEX OF POEMS BY TITLE

4.20 a.m.	165	Chris Hock	89	Hallowe'en	159
A Biblical Hero	74–5	Chuck Joseph	122	Hanky Panky	204,
A Business Scheme Involving Ducks	180	Clifford's Pen	48		249–63
A Diligent Bee	91	Commitment	207	Hospital	233
A Loaded Guy	52	Common Interests	112	Identity	235
A Proactive Man	274	Corporal Moore's Mission	30	If Only They Had Known	116
A Sad Poem	46	Courage	279	In Egypt	121
A Simple Offering	103	Cupid	102	In Leicester	205
A Touching Moment	51	Deliberately Gory Poem	222	In Nottingham	155
Abduction	200	Derreck Woods	8	Investment	33
Ag	139	Digger	149	Jelly	162
Am Dram	5	Dirty Derreck	218	Jimmy	269
An Accidental Hero	76	Donald	65	Joint Account	194
An Application	82	Double the Fun	198	Jon Snow	87
An Arctic Scene	117	Dreaming	161	Kafkaesqueish?	223
An Athlete's Woes	145	Drenched	88	Ken's Lot	238
Anyone?	277	Drive Through	129	Lazy	148
Apples	179	Dunk	184	Leafing	278
Arnold	7	Dying Wishes	43	Liberties	84
At Work	281	Enough	167	Longtermism	144
Bad Call	231	Envy	272	Love	219
Bangkok Bell-Ends	126	Flames	237	Loveboy	182–3
Batesy's Banter	4	Floater	128	Lovely Stuff	9
Big Bill Waller	174	Floods	164	Loyalty	244
Bloody Custard	176	For Ease of Licking	141	Mates' Rates	104
Boasting	175	For My Passengers' Sake	67	Maud	50
Bonker's Game	133	Freddie	72	Men and Fish	71
Borneo?	124	Fun	99	Mike's Project	188
Boss/Secretary	92	Gary	185	Miss D.H. French	79
Boys On Tour	125	Gigging	217	Moaty	140
Brown's Eye	68	God Being God	35	Most Unwelcome	245
Bugwoman	86	Going Medieval	142	Night Time	169
Capricorn	163			Norway	115
Charm	42			Not Enough	120

Not So Welcome 280
Notch 158
Occupational
    Hazard 239
Off the Cuff 195
Old Meat 234
On the Expenses
    Scandal 186–7
Online Bullshit 40
Opportunity 212
Order 143
Over 146
Paint 232
Pat vs Matt 105
Penis Eyes 221
Pitt 177
Plans 17
Plummeting 230
Poor Donna 83
Poor Form 90
PR 6
Prayer 32
Preparation 268
Public Reaction 14
Pursuit 275
Radiohead 137
Radox 166
Romance 201
Shackles 62
Sharing 271
Shopping Garrett 26
Sights 10
Silver 199
Standing by the
    Sandwiches 276
Stats 267
Sunday Morning ix
Suspicion 15
SW19 70
The Awkwardness
    of War 23
The Banter 105
The Beginning 53

The Change 240
The Cheeky
    Guardian 181
The Compliment 44
The Conference 173
The Cretan Beach 119
The Crucible 12
The Curse 202
The Date 45
The End 31
The End 270
The Furious
    Citizen 28
The Fury 220
The Futility of War 27
The Greater Good 64
The Guys 106–07
The Incident
    in Ryman's 25
The Johnny 3
The Lads 97
The Logistics
    of War 34
The Main Ant 63
The Modest
    Man with the
    Crampons 69
The Nook 109
The Overclaim 93
The Pilgrimage 118
The Plan 147
The Procedure 208
The Realities
    of War 22
The Reunion 108
The Routine
    Breaks Down 127
The Rules of War 21
The Sad Tale of
    Chris and Sian 41
The Shake-Up 80
The Sikh and
    The Christian 29
The Sonofabitch 150
The Sparrow 273

The Thick of Night 156
The Tragedy
    of Hope 54–6
The Trip 111
The Universe 168
The Valley of
    the Kings 123
The Very,
    Very Big Man 213
The Wizard 241
The Wooden Man 66
The Work Ethic 81
Threes 110
Through
    the Partition 203
Tiger 214–5
Toad 189
Together 196
Tom 178
Too Much All
    At Once 100
Too Much Chewing
    Gum in One Go 47
Trifle 197
'Twas the Snap
    Awoke Her 236
Typical Ernest 49
Untitled 11, 13, 24,
    61, 98, 138,
    151, 157,
    164, 206,
    211, 216,
    224

Up 226
Walking With
    William 225
Wandsworth 85
What Can Happen 242–3
With Vegetables 229
Wrenched 16
Yards 73

INDEX OF POEMS
BY FIRST LINE

Aaren Woogle went down the deed poll office. 240

A badger stopped working nights. 166

A centre back went to York to have sex with a referee's daughter he'd met at a dinner. 219

A Christian noticed he was good at sprinting. 24

A leg floated by. 128

A man with inwards hands . . . 269

A pop star changed her hairstyle. 14

A Sikh and a Christian traded religions . . . 29

A sparrow became obsessed with Emma Bunton. 273

A Swede farted. 173

A United States citizen got his hands on a gun. 122

A website was developed. 9

Abigail spent twelve grand on a haircut. 33

Aiden bought the girl with the kite twenty gifts. 275

Al slipped over in Bethlehem. 118

Albert wrongly analysed a situation. 231

Alistair Darling went for a shit . . . 90

All the others went to Israel. 125

All the soldiers were on the beach throwing bombs at each other. 27

Alvin West built a moat around his car whenever he parked it . . . 140

Amy licked her lips. 169

An ant broke all the carrying records. 63

Anderson set about building a ladder in order to climb over the wall. 146

Apples . . . 179

Arnold was constantly unhappy . . . 7

B.A. was bellyaching. 127

Ballard handed the waitress the menu. 143

Barry put ink on the eye bit of Mr Walker's telescope. 168

Barry went to the shops and bought everything he needed for the rest of his life. 144

Bedecked in white shawls . . . 123

Big Bill Waller . . . 174

Bill Gower got a job as a doctor's receptionist. 80

Bonker built a lasso out of fishing line. 133

Brad Pitt killed Andre Agassi. 177

Brian Hills and Ian Fisher both saw the same escort. 112

Bugwoman . . . 86

'Can I have one more crumb please?' 11

Capricorn killed Michael, Rod and the dogs. 163

Carlo . . . 64

Chad bought me the latest shirt. 103

China and America both wore blue to the war. 34

Chris and Sian started having an affair. 41

Chris darned his condom in front of his electric fire. 3

Chris hadn't seen Tania for about three years . . . 25

Chris Hock . . . 89

Chris jumped outta the plane. 230

Chris-Chris sat with Dolly for almost over an hour. 279

Christopher Pound was the hardest working of all the bees. 91

Clark kissed his wife on their first wedding anniversary. 207

Clark Watchman was an amazing mountaineer. 69

Clifford bought a pen. 48

Corporal Moore was asked to go undercover. 30

'Custard – you goddamn fool!' 176

Dave Pin-Willis ate a hundred and ten pies. 102

David – the absolutely minute boy . . . 74

Denise South . . . 239

Derreck dangled by the dunk-pot. 8

Dirty Derreck spiked a birdbath. 218

Donald bought a tent . . .	65
Donna – the receptionist – tried to eat some of her plum.	83
Edward Mark Warner took Gloria to a very plush restaurant.	184
Elizabeth put seventy packets of chewing gum in her mouth at once.	47
Elvin, Jonathan Chorus, T.T.L.R. Robertson, Ian and his new squeeze, the Willet sisters, Erica Vaughan, Tom's lot, Warren and his boyfriend (the optician, not that other arsehole), Chris, Khalid, Jessica and the old man from the cinema went on a weekend away . . .	111
For some reason everyone texted John.	100
Franz Kafka bought an orange.	223
Freddie Flintoff scored 155 runs!	72
Gareth really liked radio.	137
Gary Glitter sat on the shitter.	185
Gayle stitched all her clothes together . . .	138
Geoffrey Rider sped down the motorway.	261
God made a cloud in the shape of a famous politician taking a shit.	35
Gomez invented a new language . . .	139
Griff had a spliff.	216
Griff Spence needed a wife.	274
Gwendolin made twenty mince pies.	211
Harold didn't go to work one day.	62
Hassan juiced some papyrus and drank it on the veranda.	121
Herman grabbed Alfred by the lapels and spat.	108
'How much for the goat?'	225
'I am playing football.'	106
I counted my wife's hands.	160
I crouched with my band.	217
I dated a girl.	44
'I don't want to talk about it.'	205
I found a new nook in my house.	109
I had a dream last night.	161
I heard tell of a man who has fucked Beyonce . . .	61
I just found out someone's trying to kill me!	10
'I like jelly.'	162
'I may as well tell you, Keith—'	258
I met a guy who was six foot four and seventeen and a half stone . . .	213
'I might eat you one day.'	167
I'm in love with a girl.	267
'I'm just worried about you.'	119
'I know what you've been saying about me.'	101
'I'm not marrying that pig!'	278
I stole £400,000 . . .	52
'I think you just want another notch on your bedpost, Laurie.'	158
'It'll take a sight more than that to win me back!'	120
'I've come about the job.'	79
'I've got a business scheme.'	180
'I've killed nine people.'	175
'I want a divorce.'	253
I went into a shop and demanded a job.	82
I went up the hospital.	233
'I will not give it to you.'	238
Ian Mint groaned . . .	197
Jaap Stam found himself sat next to Aled Jones on an aeroplane.	116
Jack Manchester went to church 100 times.	32
Jack pulled his black trunks up over his belly and waded in.	115
James attempted to murder his wife.	206
Jeff (Jeff Quinn) . . .	46
Jeff Adder looked across at the couple by the window.	272
Jeremy Bailey's little plane crashed in the jungle.	124
Jimmy drank a half of Becks Vier.	269
John Cun painted all his stuff white.	232
John stared at his wife, hard.	200
John wanted to screw Maud.	50
June – the five year old – couldn't stop laughing.	76
Keith Power asked his wife why the Marmite had run out.	259
Keith Power bought candles and scallops and a banner for his wife's birthday.	260
Keith Power dangled the tie in his wife's face.	263
Keith Power drove west along Midsummer Avenue.	259
Keith Power hacked into his wife's email account.	259
Keith Power pulled off his overalls and lit his pipe.	257
Keith Power sped down the Marie Power.	262
Keith Power walked aimlessly through town.	260
Keith Power walked in on his wife as she wallowed in her bath, hippo-style.	259
Keith Power wiggled his key in the lock some more.	258
Keith Power, Marie Power and Mario Shaw relaxed in bed.	260
Keith Power, Marie Power, Mario Shaw and Cindy Shaw . . .	258
Keith was shaking the wig in his wife's face now.	259
Keith was staring at his wife's fingers.	259

Keith's shirt was smeared tight against his chest with the sweat. 259

Lee snuck off to get a crêpe and some beer. 21

Lesley Garrett frowned. 26

Lester arrived late at the orgy because of traffic. 276

'Let's get a joint account.' 194

Loveboy kissed 33 women. 182

Mandy Gandhi . . . 49

Marge scrutinised my timesheet. 93

Maria sat sobbing in her cell at the all-women's prison. 5

Marie did a shit in a cemetery. 155

Marie Power asked Keith to wear a mask during sex. 259

Marie Power gave birth. 258

Marie Power told Keith she was bored of his tracksuit top. 258

Marie Power went missing. 260

Marie Power, a class-A homewrecker, seduced Mario. 255

Mario came round. 260

Mario did some hanky-panky with his wife. 204, 249

Mario hooked his penis over his waistband and rang the bell. 258

Mario kissed his wife. 251

Mario porked 254

Mario screwed Keith Power's wife. 250

Mario Shaw offered to do Keith's kitchen. 258

Mario Shaw staggered into the bedroom . . . 259

'Mario's moving in.' 258

Mario snogged his wife. 252

Mario tried to convince Keith Power's wife to take him and Linda Goldberg's husband at the same time. 258

Martin Blousy waited under the big clock thing in Waterloo Station. 54

Matt was literally all over the place. 23

Maurice lost his wife to flu, and, some days later, found himself at a speed-dating night. 43

Me, Brendan Worth and Laura Chen . . . 110

Michael put 50p in his piggy bank every day for three years. 15

Mick Finch got to the curry last. 270

Mike shoved his dick into Caroline. 201

Mike White stole a bat from his father's cave. 188

Morne needed a pen. 53

Morris bought his wife twenty kilos of silver. 199

My future wife eyeballed me across our pancakes. 42

Nancy – a prozzie – won the lottery . . . 81

Nathan was fed up. 235

Neil Robertson (the snooker player) . . . 12

Oliver built his wife an igloo. 117

Oliver Hampton-Church . . . 22

Owing to a mixture of youth, greed and stupidity, Annie and Walker shoved a bunch of drugs up their arses . . . 126

Pat blew a bubble. 226

Pat spat on Matt. 105

Paul Loud . . . 229

Pearl slept. 148

'Penis Eyes!' 221

Pete Moore set himself up as a peeping Tom. 178

Peter told a couple of white lies and bagged himself two wives. 198

Phil Nottinghamshire tried to tip the waitress. 242

Philip Brookes practised standing in front of his mirror. 268

Philip dropped a bomb from his plane onto some foreign soldiers. 28

Pinocchio . . . 66

'Powerpoint! My man!' 260

Rat fucked Toad. 189

Richard decided to give his missus a fright on Hallowe'en night. 159

Richard Feast suddenly got into medieval things and castles. 142

Rick-Paul Burnett got an operation in an unofficial hospital . . . 141

Rob Decker's office flooded. 88

Rob Lyle had a wizard come to him. 241

Robin got in a box. 234

Robin stared into the fire. 237

Roger Federer won Wimbledon. 70

Roy caught an absolutely brilliant fish. 71

Roy said, 'Help yourself to anything' . . . 84

Roy was mowing the lawn. 222

Ruby Danzak texted: 'Who's up for it?' 277

'Scratch my back.' 104

Sean and Christine had a bath together. 196

Shawn watched the two black belts demonstrating. 17

She sat in the café. 281

Stephen Bryant . . . 147

Steve Ovett got kidnapped . . . 145

Steve West touched a breast and boasted to his mates. 51

Stripe – my faithful old dog – killed the burglar. 244

Suzie Dent and Jim Broadbent were marshalling Dictionary Corner. 181

Terry drank a yard of ale. 73

The alcoholic, Nick Webb, spends his weekends digging tunnels. 149

The beautiful blonde girl on the N15 bus on 29 January 2011 ... 164

The best man didn't prepare a speech as such. 195

The bleak businessman snapped his shoehorn ... 236

The girl who looked like Kevin Spacey ... 224

The holiday photos came back. 258

The most beautiful girl in the world ... 129

The penises in charge of the world ... 31

The Queen got shot in the guts. 212

The Queen took a normal job so the public would hate her less. 6

The vicar pored over the statistics. 202

There was a big do ... 186

There was a chap in the café highlighting his phone bill. 150

There was a gap in the track and the train was heading right for it. 67

There was an imposter in my bed. 245

There were muddy footprints going up the stairs. 258

They advertised for a new flat mate and got one called Nikki. 280

'This table's unstable!' 220

Tiger winked at the barmaid. 214

Todd started a fire. 157

Tony had his surgeon stitch a heart-shaped light to the palm of his hand ... 151, 208

Twelve bottles of champagne were delivered to the Powers'. 258

Two lesbians ... 45

Two ugly bastards ... 40

Wanda Marshall drank 100 vodkas. 99

Wandsworth – bank clerk – got told about dress-down Friday too late. 85

We clubbed together and bought an annual. 97

'Westy, you swine!' 98

'What am I doing here?' 13

'When I point to things in the studio some of them aren't actually there.' 87

'Which one's the glass one?' 68

'While you're down there ...' 4

'Why did you just call me "Mario"?' 259

'Why do you never sexually harass me?' 92

Wilson cracked a joke. 165

'You shouldn't use such a big spoon!' 203

'Your arm's jutting into my flank.' 156

INDEX OF POEMS BY THEME

A lady shouting at a head — 159

Abuse, insults, rudery et cetera — 4, 72, 98, 103, 108, 110, 150, 176, 221, 232, 236, 268, 278

Bags and sacks — 26, 104, 144, 258, 275

Bald guys (inclusive of guys in wigs) — 179, 249–56, 258, 262, 263

Barack Obama, US President extraordinaire — 68

Beasts — 10, 12, 21, 43, 51, 63, 64, 71, 86, 91, 121, 122, 123, 126, 133, 163, 166, 176, 189, 218, 242, 273

Beautiful men and women — 3, 12, 14, 32, 33, 41, 42, 43, 51, 54, 70, 71, 112, 123, 129, 147, 164, 177, 182, 214, 221, 236, 242, 267, 273, 281

Big ideas — 9, 31, 80, 117, 139, 142, 144

Big, strapping lads — 8, 17, 25, 33, 34, 35, 61, 67, 69, 72, 73, 74, 97, 115, 116, 124, 127, 133, 140, 174, 201, 213, 214, 219

Blood in various quantities and for various reasons — 5, 14, 21, 22, 23, 26, 27, 29, 64, 67, 74, 111, 118, 122, 127, 144, 159, 217, 222, 229, 244

Bright sunshine — 23, 24, 27, 98, 105, 120, 123, 128, 146, 203, 225, 258, 273

Camel illustration — 115

Cans are open or people are getting lashed — 4, 14, 73, 97, 99, 108, 161, 174, 194, 195, 202, 214, 216, 269, 270

Centre backs — 106, 116, 219

Chewy girls — 26, 47, 87, 275

Corns and calluses — 129

Crying guys — 71, 116, 124, 126, 240

Deluge — 88, 100, 164

Difficult dinners — 229

Featuring a foreign man — 12, 27, 28, 30, 64, 70, 72, 74, 111, 117, 120, 121, 125, 139, 173, 214, 223, 270

Featuring a window made out of a polycarbonate material, as opposed to glass — 167

Featuring people who are earning a fat old wedge — 6, 10, 14, 26, 33, 44, 61, 68, 70, 72, 87, 90, 93, 143, 161, 177, 181, 186, 194, 212, 214, 219, 236, 242, 273

Findus crispy pancakes — 159

Fire (natural or electric) — 3, 155, 157, 237

Frozen eyelids — 159

Golfers and tennis players — 44, 70, 177, 214

Goons losing their jobs — 79, 85

Great, great guys — 8, 17, 29, 30, 34, 35, 57, 62, 67, 71 72, 97, 117, 124, 127, 141, 166, 174, 181, 182, 186, 212, 281

Greedy sons of bitches — 52, 104, 126, 186, 198

Guys called Chris   3, 25, 41, 89, 91, 106, 111, 137, 195, 230

Guys travelling at over 100km/h   28, 116, 124, 230, 261

Guys who are actually getting on with
   something/doing something about it   17, 40, 43, 63, 117, 144, 149, 168, 186, 271, 274

Guys who are in some ways inadequate or
   have at some point had their self-esteem
   shot to pieces   24, 101, 267

Guys with a lot on their mind   3, 6, 7, 11, 33, 44, 83, 99, 101, 129, 145, 164, 204, 222, 257–9,
   272, 279

Guys with balls   67, 147, 174, 181, 212, 225

Happy girls   33, 42, 45, 49, 53, 70, 76, 81, 102, 123, 138, 148, 169, 182, 196
   199, 201, 216, 224, 258, 259

Hash and drugs and shit   124, 126, 186, 216

Having to spend time
   with an annoying wretch   6, 15, 49, 74, 120, 179, 180, 213, 232, 272

Hiding   109, 159

Hopeless romantics   3, 12, 32, 46, 48, 50, 53, 54, 62, 91, 151, 201, 207, 208, 268,
   275, 279

Horaces   23

Human activity   3–6, 8–15, 17, 21–34, 40–54, 61, 62, 64–76, 79–85, 87–90, 92,
   93, 97, 112, 115–29, 133, 137–51, 155–15, 167–69, 173–88,
   194–208, 211–26, 229–44, 249–63, 267–72, 274–81

In which a bicycle is used   46, 71, 188, 204, 205

In which the main character had
   eczema when he or she was little
   but they are okay now   43, 89, 143, 202

Inheritance   176, 242

Injustice   13, 15, 21, 28, 74, 79, 84, 101, 104, 109, 110, 125, 155, 186, 189

Involving someone physically
   outstanding   66, 74, 108, 196, 213, 214, 224

Kissing but no screwing   54, 70, 89, 169, 207, 212, 251, 252

Leafing through documents   93, 202

Liars   ix, 66, 93, 198

Lithuanian ladies   143, 242

Long, ultimately fatal, waits   54, 159

Love-making of various types   25, 40, 43, 46, 49, 50, 61, 71, 81, 112, 156, 182, 189, 197, 201,
   204, 214, 218, 219, 241, 249, 250, 257, 258, 276

Lynchings   14

Maggots and wizards   7, 241

Magnificent Eskimos   31, 117

Male nurses with a wicked sense
   of humour   159

Mid-air   28, 116, 226, 230, 273

More than eighty litres of water   23, 31, 64, 88, 90, 115, 128, 140, 196

More than forty litres of mead   142

Old folk (including politicians who
   act old and sensible so we trust them)   5, 6, 35, 50, 85, 104, 111, 119, 148, 176, 186, 202, 207, 212,
   231, 241, 268, 280

Opera singers/other singers/Emma Bunton   14, 26, 116, 273

Over-reacting wives   159

Pagan festivals   159

Pale blue faces   159

Parliamentary water   90

Partitions that slide upon two sets of runners
– one at the top and one at the bottom   198

Placing one thing into another (fingers
plunging into eyes, flags into mountains,
Lesley Garrett et cetera)   3, 15, 26, 34, 47, 67, 68, 69, 148, 201, 236, 237, 258, 271

Playwrights   4

Poems in which something is plugged in   3, 6, 14, 26, 62, 66, 83, 121 (assuming it's an electric juicer
and he's not just squeezing the stuff into a cup), 159, 161,
234, 258, 259, 267, 271

Poems set in a 'utility room' that adjoins
the kitchen and mainly contains white-
goods, sledges and rollerskates   159

Poems where the main guy is wearing a beret   32, 41, 87, 92, 142, 160, 175, 185

Posh guys   6, 22, 26, 90, 118, 143, 162, 168, 178, 184, 186, 212, 280

Practical jokes   159

Rhyming   49, 51, 185, 216, 220

Roberts radios (the old-fashioned-looking
leather ones that are secretly bang up to
date and play digital stations)   137

Second dates   201

Set in kitchens (at least in part)   84, 108, 159, 162, 165, 167, 194, 202, 216, 219, 259, 280

Set in Ryman's   25, 82

Simple-minded idiots   3, 31, 40, 47, 65, 80, 82, 85, 93, 97, 98, 105, 116, 122, 126, 140,
141, 146, 176, 180, 278

Sobbing ladies   5, 44, 83, 126, 164, 205, 242, 253, 258

Socially incapable goons   4, 5, 12, 40, 41, 66, 85, 89, 139, 140, 142, 178, 185, 223, 231,
240, 269, 277

Some guy just loses it (rightly or wrongly)   72, 84, 108, 150, 163, 175, 184, 205, 206, 220, 229

Someone eats something interesting
(including things like yoghurt and lobsters)   21, 47, 102, 124, 133, 137, 148, 177, 188, 206, 211, 229, 231,
238, 272

Someone gets a nice present   52, 91, 103, 179, 199, 259, 275

Surgery   141, 151, 208, 212

The 'Guess Who' reunion, 2005   108

The return of a wife, sixteen years after
faking her own abduction   200

The wooden piano   210

Worried or uneasy guys   7, 10, 12, 13, 23, 51, 54, 88, 89, 90, 93, 100, 101, 115, 119, 128,
158, 175, 185, 195, 231, 234, 235, 239, 240, 245, 263, 276, 277,
279, 281

Written in a taxi   178, 196

Zanussi ZQF6114A Integrated Freezer,
White   159

INDEX OF POEMS BY PEOPLE PARADING AROUND IN THEM

Adder, Jeff 272
Adobe, Chris 156
Agassi, Andre 177
Ameobi, Caroline 201
Anderson, Harold 146
Antonioni, Richard 159
Apples 179
Arterton, Lucy 269
Arthur, Lester 276
Bailey, Jeremy 124
Ballard, Captain 143
Balls, Ed 186
Baracus, B. A. 127
Barker, Sue 70
Bates, Candy 4
Bates, Mike 4
Beef, Denise 182
Bird, Rod 'Dickie' 163
Blade, Nathan 235
Blousy, Martin 54
Bogs, Warren 111
Bolt, Tony 213
Bottom, Jessica 111
Briers, Bernard 108
Broadbent, Jim 180

Brookes, Philip 268
Brookes, Sian 41
Brown, Gordon 68
Brown, Icke 106
Brundle, Miriam 182
Bryant, Stephen 147
Buckingham, Roy 84
Bugwoman 86
Bunton, Emma 273
Burnett, Rick-Paul 141
Butter, Chris-Chris 279
Cannivaro, Nancy 81
Capricorn 163
Carr, Wendy 51
Chains, Pippa 182
Chang, Michael 177
Charles, Alison 182
Charles, Rosie 182
Chase, Amy 169
Chen, Laura 110
Chorus, Jonathan 111
Christ, Jesus 125
Chung, Sally 257
Clunes, Martin 161
Cluster, Geoff 106

Cooper, Crystal 221
Cornwall, Judd 30
Cowans, Marie 155
Crutchley, Tabitha 182
Cun, John 232
Curley, Anna 46
Custard 176
Daley, Donna 83
Danzak, Ruby 277
Darling, Alistair 90
Davenport, Anita 108
De La Bona, Trudy 182
Decker, Rob 88
Delaney, Derreck 218
Delfini, Anne 54
Dennis, Jimmy 269
Dennis, Oliver 117
Dent, Susie 181
Derreck, Glass 17
Dew, Pat 226
Dott, Graham 12
Downes, Roy 222
Downing,
Gayle Laura 138
Dunn, Bill 108

Durham, Regina 182
Edinburgh, Duke o' 6
Evans, Maurice 43
Evans, Victoria 43
Face 127
Farrow, Roo 182
Feast, Richard 142
Federer, Roger 70
Few, Gladys 182
Finch, Mick 270
Fisher, Ian 112
Flintoff, Freddie 72
Force, Muriel 182
Forrest, Clark 207
Fox, Claire 200
Fox, John 200
Fraser, Pat 105
French, Miss D. H. 79
Gabrielle 55
Garrett, Lesley 26
Garribaldi, Aiden 275
Gath, Goliath of 74
George, Chloe 211
Gandhi, Mandy 49
Glitter, Gary 185
God 35
Goldberg, Linda 258
Gomez, Andersson 139
Gorringe, Matt 23
Gower, Bill 80
Grade, Luther 203
Graf, Steffi 177
Graham, Liz 89
Green, Rachel 257
Greer, Peter 108
Greer, Suzan 108
Grey, Mr 83
Groves, Annie 126
Hall, Nicky 66
Hampton-Church, Oliver 22
Harmison, Steve 72
Hassan, Hassan 121
Hastings, Horace 23
Hawkins, Sally 258
Hayden, Clara 3
Heart, Connie 268
Higgins, Helen 128

Highgate, Griff 101
Hills, Brian 112
Hock, Chris 89
Hoon, Geoff 186
Howard, Ernest 49
Huggins, Maud 50
Hughes, David 74
Humphries, Horace 238
Hurst, Michael 15
Hussain, Nasser No mention
II, Queen Elizabeth 6, 212
Ince, Donald 65
James, Chris 111
Jessop, Bod 109
Jones, Aled 116
Kafka, Franz 223
Kerr, Philip 28
Kinsella, Maud 182
Kitinka, Maria 5
Knight, Ken 238
Knowles, Beyonce 61
Krasić, Branco 270
Lacey, Karen 44
Lamarr, Kiki 182
Lancaster, Ms Nikki 280
Lawson, Nicki 84
Leighton, Lee 21
Lenin, Clifford 48
Lewis, Chris 25
Loud, Paul 229
Louisiana, Diane 157
Louisiana, Lou 182
Lowe, Ethan 106
Lowe, Jack 115
Lowe, Margaret 13
Lyle, Daphne 241
Lyle, Rob 241
Lynagh, Elizabeth 47
Lynam, Des 181
Maids, Des 230
Maine, Gwendolin 211
Manchester, Jack 32
Marsden, Connie 182
Marsh, Cruella 182
Marshall, Alan 27
Marshall, Richard 27
Marshall, Wanda 99
Mates, Stephanie 182

Matthews, Michael 163
Maxwell, Chris 41
McFadden, Steve 260
McGrath, Glenn 72
McGregor, Elaine 182
Michael 218
Michaels, Tania 25
Mild, Chris 106
Miliband, David 187
Miliband, Ed 187
Ministry, Brigitte 198
Ministry, Maggie 198
Ministry, Peter 198
Mint, Ian 197
Mint, Jenny 197
Moorcroft, Esther 274
Moore, Dave 30
Moore, Pete 178
Morden, Todd 157
Morrissey, Neil 161
Mound, Laurie 158
Mulberry, Ian 111
Murdock, Captain H. M. 127
Myers, Kerry 108
Nottinghamshire1 Phil 242
O'Connor, Des 181
O'Leary, Marge 93
Obama, Barack 68
Old, Annie 182
Oldham, Callie of 182
Otto 123
Ovett, Steve 145
Page, Stan 101
Page, Tone 101
Palmer, Malc 104
Paulini, Benjamin 17
Perkins, Nora 89
Philips, Andy 176
Pickles, Perry 179
Pin-Willis, Dave 102
Pinocchio 66
Pitt, Brad 177
Point, John 100
Pontefract, Dolly 279
Porterhome, Ben 119
Porthos, Robin 234
Pound, Christopher 91

Power, Keith   204, 249, 250,
                      251, 252, 253,
                      255, 257, 258,
                      259, 261, 262
Power, Marie   255, 257, 258,
                      259, 261
Proud, Anneka
Rose-Marie   182
Pugh, Marianne   182
Purvis, Si   217
Pushkin, Bonker   133
Quill, Gloria   182
Quinne, Jeff   46
Rainer, Khalid   111
Range, Greg   71
Rat   189
Raymond, Karen   89
Reagan, Anne   258
Reagan, Barry   258
Reddoor, Louise   151, 208
Redmond, Jim   46
Rib, John   101
Roberts, Genevieve   48
Roberts, Mrs   182
Robertson, Neil   12
Robertson, T.T.L.R.   111
Roseberry, Stewart   106
Rosenthal, Ronnie   125
Rossi, Carlo   64
Rougerie, Tom   108
Ruby   176
Rudolfini, Yvonne   182
Ryder, Geoffrey   261
Santilli, Chad   103
Shaw, Cindy   258
Shaw, Mario   204, 249, 250
                      251, 252, 253,
                      254, 255, 258,
                      259, 261
Shepherd, Morne   53
Slide, James T.   206
Smart, Robert   108
Smith, Hannibal   127
Smith, Harold   62

Smith, Ian 'Eggsy'   270
Snow, Jon   87
South, Denise   239
Spacey, Kevin   224
Spence, Griff   274
Spirit, Matt   105
Staines, Robin   237
Stam, Jaap   116
Stamp, Lewis   101
Stančiūtė, Eliza   242
Stark, Mike   201
Stelling, Jeff   181
Stewart, Claire   232
Stewart, Elaine   34
Stewart, Eric   108
Stone, Paulette   182
Stout, Wandsworth   85
Strachan, Tony   151, 208
Straw, Jack   186
Stripe   244
Stump, Barry   168
Swallow, Winston   106
Swann, Christine   196
Swann, Sean   196
Tabb, Michaela   12, 55
Tandy, Candy   182
Tang, Barry   144
Taylor, Chris   3
Taylor, Griff   216
Taylor, Mandy   216
Taylor, Terry   73
Temple, Lou   182
Toad   189
Tongue, Gladys   102
Topsy, Morris   199
Towns, Gareth   137
Troy, Roy   71
Turban, Winkie   240
Turnball, Gloria   184
Vaughan, Erica   111
Vein, Al   118

Waddle, Herman   108
Wade, Elvin   111
Wainwright, Abigail   33
Walker, Sir Adam   168
Walker, Willie   126
Wallace, Arnold   7
Waller, Big Bill   174
Ward, Bert   270
Warne, Albert   231
Warne, Shane   72
Warner,
Edward Mark   184
Warzycha, Chris   230
Watchman, Clark   69
Webb, Cynthia   182
Webb, Nick   149
Welch, Ron   100
West, Alfred   108
West, Alvin   140
West, Jim   98
West, Steve   51
Westwood, Lee   44
White, Mike   188
Whitely, Richard   181
Widdecombe, Ann   186
Wilde, Rod   109
Willet, Christine   111
Willet, Honour   111
William   225
Wilson, Nicola   165
Wilson, P.   165
Winslett, Gayle   148
Woods, Derreck   8
Woods, Larry   180
Woods, Tiger   214
Woogle, Aaren   240
Worth, Brendan   110
Worthing, John   50
Yates, Laura   213
Yorke, June   76
York, Mrs   144

INDEX OF POEMS BY NUMBER

Poem	Page	Poem	Page	Poem	Page	Poem	Page
33	120	430	213	618	116	838	28
83	149	444	4	621	232	841	201
96	79	445	5	622	66	850	133
112	10	449	128	624	147	863	68
114	119	466	173	631	181	869	87
142	233	467	44	636	160	880	105
146	97	471	177	645	127	891	277
149	45	475	51	651	274	893	180
159	244	476	237	677	185	894	268
171	278	477	157	679	23	895	241
180	217	479	71	680	27	897	184
185	138	486	108	681	21	898	129
206	204, 249–63	487	81	684	22	900	100
221	197	491	48	688	86	908	12
229	42	492	230	705	54–6	913	182–3
250	109	495	72	708	279	918	142
258	225	505	272	710	179	919	267
262	156	516	148	714	3	922	33
269	85	517	115	716	220	926	165
272	167	520	17	723	218	935	65
286	203	522	240	726	275	938	88
324	29	525	145	733	175	940	137
329	24	527	235	736	216	941	80
332	205	528	62	746	74–5	942	14
335	32	531	46	750	91	943	83
341	84	536	222	751	69	948	40
362	200	538	281	764	169	950	242–3
369	117	567	150	770	8	962	269
387	82	572	118	780	163	963	90
394	111	575	76	785	139	969	121
400	16	577	101	786	106	982	47
401	238	578	110	806	89	983	211
406	99	579	221	807	104	994	15
412	123	584	26	811	52	1000	231
416	125	597	70	813	194	1004	7
421	239	603	50	824	49	1010	30
427	161	613	102	830	98	1012	219
429	112	615	13	834	176	1031	151
		617	103	836	162	1031	208

Poem	Page	Poem	Page
1035	140	1183	31
1038	214-5	1184	43
1052	186	1186	195
1060	146	1189	61
1062	199	1190	73
1063	226	1193	67
1069	143	1196	126
1070	11	1991	245
1071	189		
1078	236		
1087	234		
1095	35		
1099	206		
1100	273		
1101	25		
1102	178		
1105	141		
1106	229		
1109	92		
1112	159		
1128	53		
1129	41		
1134	155		
1136	212		
1139	223		
1141	224		
1142	144		
1146	158		
1147	280		
1148	196		
1149	122		
1150	124		
1151	63		
1152	174		
1153	93		
1155	6		
1159	188		
1160	168		
1163	64		
1166	198		
1167	207		
1169	202		
1172	276		
1174	271		
1177	9		
1178	270		
1179	164		
1180	166		
1182	34		

ACKNOWLEDGEMENTS

I think I should thank these people:

Hannah Begbie, Kitty Laing, Simon Trewin,
Ariella Feiner, Stephen Merchant,
Simon Pearce, Nick Davies, Norah Perkins,
everyone at Canongate, the lady in the café,
Phillip Breen, Peter Le May, Bill Key,
Carol Key, Seb Antoniou, and the guys
at The Community Centre.

These people gave me inspiration,
accommodation, pens, deskspace,
drive and love.

CANON █ GATE.tv

CHANNELLING GREAT CONTENT

WATCH — INTERVIEWS, TRAILERS, ANIMATIONS, READINGS, GIGS

LISTEN — AUDIO BOOKS, PODCASTS, MUSIC, PLAYLISTS

READ — CHAPTERS, EXCERPTS, SNEAK PEEKS, RECOMMENDATIONS

DISCOVER — BLOGS, EVENTS, NEWS, CREATIVE PARTNERS

SHOP — LIMITED EDITIONS, BUNDLES, SECRET SALES